MATTHEW

from
The Last Days Bible

From cousin Jim
Please read –
eternity is a long time
to end up in the wrong
place.
Caring for you,
Love Jim

MATTHEW from The Last Days Bible

It is the intent and desire of the publishers of this vibrant new translation of the Holy Scriptures that everyone feel free to quote or reprint from it without the necessity of obtaining prior written permission. Therefore, permission is hereby granted to one and all to quote and reprint up to one thousand (1,000) verses from the Last Days Bible, together with footnotes if desired. However, the 1,000 verses and footnotes must comprise less than 50% of an entire book of the bible, and must amount to less than 50% of the book or other work in which they are quoted.

A proper line of copyright credit must appear on the title or copyright page or at the point of copy of any work quoting from The Last Days Bible, as follows:

Scriptures quoted from The Last Days Bible, Copyright © 1994 by Life Messengers, Seattle, Washington 98111-1967. Used by permission.

In less formal documents such as Sunday School and youth materials, church bulletins, newsletters, reports, posters, transparencies, electronic bulletin boards, magazine articles, and all similar material, the letters LDB at the end of each quote will be sufficient.

Quotations of more than 1,000 verses, or other permission requests, must be directed to and approved in writing by Life Messengers before use.

ISBN 0-9642470-0-3

Published by
Life Messengers, Seattle, WA 98111-1967
Printed in U.S.A.

These Are The Facts

Fact one: Wake up! Wake up! The King is coming! The end of this age is fast approaching, and most of the world is fast asleep to the fact. In this captivating, new translation of Matthew, you will find vital notes of explanation on the prophetic scriptures. We deal with some 58 prophetic sections throughout the New Testament. Some of these are brief prophecies, while others are whole chapters. In The Revelation, the last book in the New Testament, we have an entire book of prophecy. In Matthew, which you hold in your hand, we deal with Bible prophecy in the entire 24th and 25th chapters. We believe the notes included, together with the appendixes for these chapters, will be of great help to you. As you read this report by Matthew, you will realize that the end is indeed fast approaching.

Fact two: Since the end is so near we need to be studying God's message to man as never before. And the same goes for your whole family, your neighbors, and everyone else. You hold in your hands an outstanding new translation of Matthew, the first book in the New Testament. As fine as other translations are, we have felt for some time the need for a new translation that flows freely, that grabs the attention and makes fascinating reading, that is absolutely correct in its translation, and that talks to us in today's way of speaking. God has a vital message for man, and it must be presented in the most correct, understandable, and interesting manner possible. We believe God has given us just such a translation. The rest of the New Testament in this translation is nearing completion, and may be in print by the time you read this. Call your bookstore.

Fact three: Besides the notes you will find here on prophecy, you will find many other notes. In fact, most of the notes are on subjects other than prophecy. But you will discover that most of these other notes pertain to Scriptures concerning our salvation. The reason for this is as follows:

About a year after beginning this translation, the editor of this project was awakened one morning about three o'clock—not sleepy awake, but wide awake. Then in a very special way God told him, "Build an evangelistic center into the translation you are working on."

So that's the reason you will find these footnotes and appendixes dealing mainly with the salvation of our soul. We believe the Lord has been with us in these writings, and we trust you will take them as from the Lord. There are warnings, words of encouragement, and words of explanation. We trust that these notes will help both you and yours to make sure of heaven.

***

Some may feel we have emphasized the necessity of obedience to God too much in these notes. But it was because of our disobedience that Christ needed to suffer and die to save us! And to be saved we must repent (turn from all our sin and obey God) as well as trust in Jesus as our Savior. Otherwise we are not converted.

But it's the repentance message that's being watered down, explained away, and omitted in much of the preaching today. We are living in the last days, when a soft, comforting message is being demanded by an unregenerate audience. See 2 Timothy 4:3-4.

Fact four: The Greek text from which we have made this translation is the Textus Receptus, commonly called the Received Text. It is called the Received Text because this was the Greek text of the New

Testament accepted by scholars hundreds of years ago as the correct Greek text. This was the Greek text from which the King James translation was made.

In recent years claims have been made that older texts have been discovered which are more reliable. We do not agree with the reliability of the so-called older texts. For a full and complete explanation regarding the reliability of the Received Text we encourage you to read the book entitled *The Identity of The New Testament Text*, by Wilbur N. Pickering, published by Thomas Nelson Publishers. Another very informative book on the subject is *Unholy Hands On The Bible*, by John W. Burgon.

Fact five: Twelve Greek scholars have given critical guidance in the forming of this translation, as well as several English purists who gave counsel in regard to style and grammar. Most of the Greek scholars are presently teaching Greek in a Christian university, seminary, or Bible school. Some have recently retired. They are godly men representing various denominations.

We are indeed grateful for all the work that all these people of God have put into this endeavor.

Fact six: Throughout the New Testament we direct you to other scriptures and notes. Those directions have been left in Matthew even though you will not be able to turn to the notes until you have the full New Testament. Likewise, there are 49 appendixes, but only the nine that pertain to Matthew have been included, besides appendix 245.

Fact seven: No effort has been made to please any person or persons, any denomination or denominations. Our only concern has been to please our Lord God by presenting a most accurate and invigorating translation, and to present notes that will be both helpful and challenging. May God be honored in all the results from the publication and dissemination of this translation of His Holy Word.

Fact eight: How can you get to heaven–for sure? You will find the answer as you read through this translation of Matthew. But we have presented a summary of the answer for you in Appendix 245, entitled, *The Amazing Story of God*. As you find the very help you need in reading this story, we trust you will share *The Amazing Story* with many.

God's main reasons for inspiring His servants to write The New Testament was to bring honor to His name and to bring us all to be with Himself forever. So be it!

Your comments or suggestions regarding this translation will be both helpful and greatly appreciated. Our fax number is 206-488-7887

Table of Contents

A Beginning Word

Jesus of Nazareth is by far the greatest Man the world has ever known. And it's no wonder He stood out so brilliantly, because it was revealed that He was earth's rightful King, the majestic Creator God! Although His public ministry lasted only three years in an obscure corner of the Roman Empire two thousand years ago, His profound influence world-wide is still without comparison. No life ever lived was more significant, no death and its results more meaningful.

Many hundreds of years after the creation of the world, God inspired dedicated men to write what we now call the Holy Bible. It was written by many authors over a period of some 1,500 years. The Bible is divided into two sections, the Old Testament and the New Testament. The Old Testament consists of the writings of Moses, David, Isaiah, Daniel, and many other prophets. After the birth, life, death, and resurrection of Jesus Christ–the promised Messiah of the Old Testament–Jesus' followers wrote the section we call the New Testament.

The New Testament tells the story of Jesus the Messiah, His instructions and warnings to His followers, the early days of His Church, and what we can expect to see happen on earth in the last days of this age just prior to His triumphant return.

This book, the book of Matthew, is the first book of the New Testament. You hold in your hands a very special new translation of Matthew for these end time days with special notes to clearly point out what God has actually done for you, and what He now expects of you if you are to escape His judgment and live forever in total fulfillment with Him. The Amazing Story of God, beginning on page 71, describes God's plan and purpose for you personally.

May this book open for you a new and marvelous relationship between you and your Creator that will result in your everlasting joy and fulfillment.

THE GREAT NEWS
as reported by
MATTHEW

The first 17 verses of Matthew contain the genealogy of Jesus the Messiah. It is suggested that (as wonderful and important as it is that we have the complete genealogy of the Messiah) you not feel obliged to read this long list of names, but begin with the story, beginning with verse 18.

These are the ancestors of Jesus the
Messiah, who came through the families of
King David and Abraham:
2 Abraham was the father of Isaac,
Isaac, the father of Jacob,
Jacob, of Judah and his brothers,
3 Judah, of Perez and Zerah, whose mother
was Tamar.
Perez was the father of Hezron,
Hezron, the father of Ram,
4 Ram, of Amminadab,
Amminadab, of Nahshon; and
Nahshon, of Salmon.
5 Salmon was the father of Boaz, whose
mother was Rahab.
Boaz was the father of Obed, whose mother was Ruth,
Obed the father of Jesse; and
6 Jesse was the father of David, who became
king.
King David was the father of Solomon, whose mother had been Uriah's wife,
7 Solomon, the father of Rehoboam,
Rehoboam, of Abijah,
Abijah, of Asa,
8 Asa, of Jehoshaphat,
Jehoshaphat, of Joram; and
Joram, of Uzziah.
9 Uzziah was the father of Jotham,
Jotham, the father of Ahaz,
Ahaz, of Hezekiah,
10 Hezekiah, of Manasseh,
Manasseh, of Amon; and
Amon, of Josiah.
11 Josiah was the father of Jeconiah and his
brothers about the time they were carried into Babylon.
12 After they had been exiled into Babylon
Jeconiah was the father of Shealtiel,
Shealtiel, of Zerubbabel,
13 Zerubbabel, of Abiud,
Abiud, of Eliakim,
Eliakim, of Azor,
14 Azor, of Zadok,
Zadok, of Achim,
Achim, of Elihud,
15 Elihud, of Eleazar,
Eleazar, of Matthan; and
Matthan, of Jacob.
16 Jacob was the father of Joseph, the husband
of Mary, who gave birth to Jesus who is called
the Messiah.[a]
17 So there were fourteen generations from
Abraham to David, fourteen from David to the captivity in Babylon, and fourteen from the captivity in Babylon to the coming of the Messiah.

18 The birth of Jesus, the long-awaited
Messiah,[a] took place in a most miraculous way. His mother, Mary, was engaged to be married to Joseph. But before they were married and had lived together, she was told by an angel of the Lord that she would soon have a baby by God's Holy Spirit.[b]
19 But Joseph, her fiancé, thought she had
sinned.[a] He was a man who wanted to do the right thing, but he didn't want to disgrace her publicly,[b] so he decided to quietly break off the engagement.
20 But as he was seriously getting ready to do
this, an angel of the Lord came to him in a dream and said, "Joseph, descendant of David, don't be reluctant about taking Mary as your wife, because the baby she will have has been conceived in her by the Holy Spirit.[a]

1:16,18a *Messiah* is Hebrew for the *Anointed One,* referring to the anointed King of Israel. *Christ* is the Greek translation.

1:18b See Luke 1:26-38.

1:19a ... *when he saw her three months later after she returned from her visit to her cousin Elizabeth.* Luke 1:26-56.

1:19b ... *by having her stoned to death* ... Leviticus 20:10, *or publicly divorcing her* ...

1:20a No doubt Joseph had confronted Mary about the baby, and she had told him about the angel coming to her, and his message. Luke 1:26-38. But Joseph didn't believe her until the angel spoke to him in a

21 "She will give birth to a Son, and you are to
name Him Jesus,[a] because He will save His
people from their sins."[b]
22 Now all this happened so that what the
Lord had announced many centuries earlier
through the prophet Isaiah, would come true,
when He said:
23 "Listen! A virgin will become pregnant and
give birth to a Son. And they will call Him
Immanuel!"[a]
which means *God is now with us!*
24 So when Joseph woke up, he did what the
angel of the Lord had told him to do, and he
and Mary were married.
25 But he had no sexual union with her until
she gave birth to her firstborn Son. And he
named Him Jesus.

Visitors from the East

2 Shortly after Jesus was born in Bethlehem
in Judea, while Herod was king, some wise
men from the East arrived in Jerusalem.
2 "Where is the Child who has been born to
be King of the Jews?" they inquired. "We saw
His star in our homeland in the East, and have
come to worship Him."
3 When King Herod heard this, he, like
everyone else in Jerusalem, was deeply shaken
by the news.
4 He called a meeting of the entire Jewish
Council, and asked them, "Where is the
Messiah[a] to be born?"
5 "In Bethlehem, in Judea," they replied,
"because this is what the prophet Micah wrote:
6 'But you, Bethlehem, though you are only
a small town in the land of Judah, you are
by no means less important than the leading cities of Judah, because out of you will
come a Ruler who will be the Shepherd of
My people Israel.'[a]"
7 Herod then secretly called the wise men to
a meeting, and questioned them carefully as to
when they had first seen the star.
8 Then he sent them to Bethlehem, after
telling them, "Go and make a most careful
search for the young child, and when you find
him, come back and tell me, so that I may go
and worship him too."
9 After their meeting with the king they went
on their way. And look! There was the same
star they had seen in the East!
10 They were ecstatic upon seeing the star
again. And it went on ahead of them until it hov-
ered over the place where the young Child was.
11 When they had entered the house,[a] there
they saw the young Child with Mary, His mother.
Falling to their knees they worshiped Him; and
opening their treasures, they presented Him with
gifts of gold, frankincense, and myrrh.

The Escape to Egypt

12 When the wise men returned home they
went another way, because God had warned
them in a dream not to go back to Herod.
13 Then think of this! After the wise men had
left, Joseph again saw an angel of the Lord in a
dream, who said, "Get up! Escape with the
young Child and His mother into Egypt! Stay
there until I tell you to return, because Herod
will soon be searching for the Child to kill Him."
14 So he got right up, and, in the middle of the
night, he took the Child and His mother and left
for Egypt, where they stayed until Herod died.
15 This took place so that the prophecy the
Lord had spoken by the prophet Hosea would
come true, when He said, "I have called My
Son out of Egypt."[a]

The Massacre of the Children

16 When Herod realized he had been outwit-
ted by the wise men, he was furious. Acting on
the information he had earlier received from
them, he sent soldiers to put to death all the
boys two years of age[a] and under in
Bethlehem and in the surrounding area.
17 Herod's bloody massacre brought about

---

dream.

1:21a The name Jesus means Savior.

1:21b Many seem to wish somehow to be *His people,* but they do not quite desire to be saved from their sins. They wish to be saved only from the *consequences* of their sins. Any *salvation* that does not save one *from* sinning, as well as from the consequences, is a delusion. One cannot be a part of *His people* while giving his allegiance to the world and the satisfying of wrongful desires.

1:23a Isaiah 7:14.

2:4a A great Deliverer (the Messiah) had been promised Israel by God many centuries before.

2:6a Micah 5:2.

2:11a Jesus was born in a cattle shed. Luke 2:7. But evidently when people heard of the baby born in a shed, a family opened their home to them. That's why the wise men from the East found the baby Jesus in a house when they arrived.

2:15a Hosea 11:1.

2:16a Because of the wording here, some claim that Jesus must have been two years old when the wise men came. But that's not good reasoning. It is very unlikely that Mary and Joseph would have stayed on in

the fulfillment of the prophecy by Jeremiah the prophet, who had said:

18 "There are screams of soul-piercing anguish, and weeping and utterly uncontrolled mourning coming from Ramah. What you are hearing is Rachel,[a] hysterically weeping for her children, refusing to be comforted, because they are dead!"[b]

The Return Home to Nazareth

19 But after Herod died, an angel of the Lord came to Joseph in a dream in Egypt.

20 "When you get up in the morning," the angel said, "take the young Child and His mother back into Israel, because those who were trying to kill Him are now dead."

21 So when he awoke he immediately got up and brought the Child and His mother back to Israel.

22 But when he heard that Herod's son Archelaus had succeeded his father as king of Judea, he was afraid to go there. After receiving further instructions from God in a dream, he withdrew[a] from Judea and went up into the region of Galilee.

23 He settled his family there in a town called Nazareth. This fulfilled the prediction of the prophets who had said, "Messiah will be called a Nazarene."

John the Baptizer Prepares the Way

3 Years later John the Baptizer went into the wilderness wasteland of Judea and preached.

2 "Turn away from your sinning, and obey God!" he warned the people again and again. "Because the Kingdom of heaven has now come very close to us!"

3 John was the man the prophet Isaiah had told about centuries before when he had said:

"Listen! Someone is shouting in the wilderness, 'Prepare for the coming of the Lord! Straighten out your ways for Him!'"[a]

4 As for John, his clothes were made of coarse, cheap camel's hair. He wore a wide leather belt around his waist, and ate locusts and wild honey.

5 From Jerusalem, from all over Judea, and from the whole region along the Jordan River, people streamed out to hear him.

6 When they openly declared that they were giving up their sinning,[a] John baptized them in the Jordan River.

7 But when John saw many of the Pharisees and Sadducees coming to where he was baptizing,[a] he challenged them, "You children of snakes! Who told you that you could escape God's fierce anger and the judgment that's coming?

8 "If you expect God to forgive you, live your life now in a way that will prove you have indeed turned from your sinning!

9 "Don't think you are safe just because you can say, 'Abraham is our ancestor,' because I'm telling you that God is able to take even these stones and raise up descendants for Abraham[a]!

10 "The axe of God's judgment is already lifted high, ready to strike at the root of the trees. And every tree that is not producing good fruit will be cut down and thrown into the fire[a]!

11 "Yes, I baptize[a] you people in water as a

Bethlehem more than a few days after Jesus was born before heading back home. What evidently happened was that very shortly after Mary and Joseph had taken Jesus to the temple (Luke 2:22-39), they were visited by the wise men. Then following that they were immediately directed to take Jesus to Egypt. The reason Herod ordered all boys two years of age and under be put to death was because he didn't want his soldiers to misjudge Jesus' age and pass him up. He felt sure to get him if he put the two-year limit. If the wise men had come when Jesus was two years of age, Herod no doubt would have put the age limit much higher than two years.

2:18a Rachel was buried near Bethlehem, and she is represented figuratively here as rising from her grave to lament with screams of soul-piercing anguish, the slaughter by Herod. She no doubt represented the many mothers in Israel who had lost their little sons, and were now weeping and wailing hysterically.

2:18b Jeremiah 31:15.

2:22a He evidently withdrew to the south, and then turned east, and traveled around the south end of the Dead Sea. From there he took the family north to Galilee. Or, he could have turned west, and then up the coast along the Mediterranean Sea.

3:3a Isaiah 40:3.

3:6a Sin – anything morally wrong, or disobedience to God, parents, the State, etc.

3:7a They came to look, to see what was going on, but they refused to be affected by his preaching or to be baptized. Luke 7:30.

3:9a The saying is true that *God has no grandchildren*. No one becomes a child of God just because of godly parents or other ancestors. The same is true for Jews.

3:10a John 15:1-16.

3:11a The original Greek word for baptize is *baupto*, and means *to dip, to immerse*.

sign that you have now changed your mind and intend to live a new life, a life that is pleasing to God. But the One who will come after me is far more powerful than I am. I'm not fit to even carry His sandals. He will baptize[a] you in the Holy Spirit and in fire.

12 "His threshing fork is already in His hand, and He will separate all the wheat from the chaff. Then He will bring His wheat into His barn,[a] but He will burn the chaff with fire that can never be put out."[b]

The Baptism of Jesus

13 Then Jesus left Galilee and went to the Jordan River where John was. He wanted John to baptize Him.

14 But John tried to talk Him out of it, saying, "Look, I need to be baptized by You,[a] and You come to me?"

15 "Just do it now," Jesus replied, "because it's the right thing for us to do, in order to fully please and obey God." So John agreed.

16 As soon as Jesus was baptized, He walked up out of the water. Then John saw a most remarkable happening: The heavens opened up! And he saw the Spirit of God come down like a dove, and come to rest upon Jesus[a]!

17 Then a voice from heaven said, "This is My Son, whom I love so dearly. I am so highly pleased with Him."

Jesus Is Tempted

4 Then the Holy Spirit led Jesus into the wilderness to allow the devil to test Him.[a]

2 After eating nothing for forty days and forty nights, He was hungry.

3 The tempter then came to Him and said, "If you are the Son of God, why don't you command these stones to become loaves of bread?"

4 But Jesus responded, "The Scriptures declare,

> 'It is not possible for man to survive on bread[a] alone. He must also feast and meditate upon every word that comes from God.'[b]"

5 Then the devil took Him into Jerusalem, and had Him stand on the highest part of the temple.

6 "Now," the devil said, "if you are the Son of God, jump down from here. According to Scripture:

> 'God will instruct His angels concerning You. They are to keep a firm hold on You with their hands, so that not even Your feet will be injured on the stones below.'[a]"

7 "But the Scriptures also say," Jesus replied, 'You must not try to force your God into a situation where He must prove Himself.'[a]"

8 Finally, the devil took Him to the top of a very high mountain and pointed out to Him all the nations of the world and their splendor.

9 "I will give you all these nations and their glory," he promised Jesus, "if you will just kneel and worship me."

10 "Satan, get out of My presence!" Jesus thundered. "The Scriptures command,

> 'You shall worship the Lord, your God, and He is the only One you shall serve!'[a]"

11 When Jesus said that, Satan left Him. Then angels came and waited on Him.

Jesus Begins His Work

12 When Jesus heard that John had been thrown into jail, He went back to Galilee.

13 But He soon moved from Nazareth to Capernaum, a city on the shores of Lake Galilee, in the area of Zebulun and Naphtali.

14 This fulfilled Isaiah's prophecy:

> 15 "Those who live in darkness[a] in the area of Zebulun and Naphtali, beside the lake and beyond the Jordan River, in the area of Galilee that is occupied by many foreigners — have seen a great light!
>
> 16 Yes, light has dawned in the region that was formerly in the dark shadow of death."[a]

17 That was when Jesus began preaching. And His message was, "Turn from your sinning to obeying God, because the Kingdom of heaven has now come very close to you!"

An Invitation to Four Fishermen

18 As Jesus was walking along the shore of

3:12a Heaven.

3:12b See Mark 9:44-48 note.

3:14a John didn't yet know that Jesus was the Messiah (see verses 16-17 and John 1:31-34), but they were second cousins (Luke 1:5-56), and John had undoubtedly been deeply impressed for years by Jesus' complete dedication to God.

3:16a John 1:29-34.

4:1a Mark 1:12 indicates this happened *immediately* after Jesus' baptism.

4:4a *Bread* here includes all material food. It can also refer to much more than just food.

4:4b Deuteronomy 8:3. Bread alone does not fill a person's need. We must also feast, meditate on, and store away in our minds and hearts, *every word* that God has given us.

4:6a Psalm 91:11-12.

4:7a Deuteronomy 6:16.

4:10a Deuteronomy 6:13.

4:15a ... *in great ignorance of God and of their relationship to Him* ...

4:15,16a Isaiah 9:1-2.

Lake Galilee one day, He saw two commercial
fishermen throw a large net out into the lake; they
were Simon, called Peter, and his brother Andrew.
19 "Come along with Me," Jesus invited them,
"and I will teach you how to harvest people
instead of fish."
20 They immediately left their nets and went
with Him.
21 As He walked farther up the beach, He saw
two other brothers, James and John, who were in a
boat with their father Zebedee, mending their nets.
He invited these brothers to come with Him too.
22 Without any hesitation, they too left the
boat and their father, and went with Him.

Jesus Teaches, Preaches, and Heals

23 Then Jesus traveled all over Galilee, teaching in their synagogues, preaching the Great
News about the Kingdom,[a] and healing every
sickness and disease among the people.
24 News about Him even spread all over
Syria. People brought Him all who were sick–
those who suffered from various diseases and
pain, the demon-possessed, the epileptics, and
those paralyzed—and He healed them all.
25 Huge crowds followed Him, coming from all
over Galilee, Decapolis, Jerusalem, Judea, and
even from the other side of the Jordan River.

The Sermon on the Mount

5 When Jesus saw the great crowds, He
went up on a hillside and sat down.
Those following Him came too,
2 and He began to teach them, saying:

Great Happiness Promised

3 "There is great happiness, both now and forever, for those who are poor in spirit,[a] because the Kingdom of heaven belongs to them!

4 There is great happiness, both now and forever, for those who mourn,[a] because they will be comforted!

5 There is great happiness ahead for those who are meek,[a] because they will inherit the earth![b]

6 There is great happiness ahead for those who hunger and thirst with desire to do what pleases God,[a] because they will be completely fulfilled!

7 There is great happiness ahead for those who are merciful to others, because they will receive mercy from God![a]

8 There is great happiness ahead for those whose hearts are pure, because it is they who will see God!

9 There is great happiness ahead for those who work for peace,[a] because it is they who will be called children of God!

10 There is great happiness, both now and for ever, for those who are persecuted because they do and say what they know is pleasing to God,[a] because the Kingdom of heaven belongs to them![b]

11 There is indeed great happiness coming your way when people insult and perse-

---

4:23a *The Kingdom* refers to both the Kingdom of God in heaven and God's Kingdom on earth. If we expect to be in His Kingdom in heaven we must turn from our sinning and rebellion, and serve and obey Him now as our Lord and King on earth.

5:3a To be poor in spirit is to have a *humble* opinion of ourselves; to fully realize what sinners we are, and that there is no way that we can save ourselves. It is to be willing to be saved only by God's rich grace and mercy, and then to be willing to do what God wants us to do, to say what He wants us to say, to be where God wants us to be, to go where He wants us to go. It means to die to all selfish ambitions for ourselves, and to come alive to God's plans and desires for us. It is to such people that Jesus promises heaven.

5:4a ... *mourning with those who mourn, but especially mourning over our sin, and over all sin, which so dishonors God ...*

5:5a Meekness is not an inferiority complex, nor a surrender of our rights, nor cowardice. It is strength under control. It is the receiving of injuries with a belief that God will vindicate us. Romans 12:19; 1 Corinthians 6:7; 1 Peter 2:19-22. And *they will inherit the earth* and reign with Christ over it. 2 Timothy 2:12; Revelation 2:26-27; 5:10.

5:5b Psalm 37; Revelation 21:7.

5:6a ... *at all times and in every situation, not choosing to neglect or ignore anything that is God's desire or command ...*

5:7a For a graphic picture of the truth of this statement by Christ, read the account of the Judgment in chapter 25, verses 31-46. The only reason given why those on his right hand receive mercy is because they have shown mercy to Jews and followers of Christ. Also read the note there.

5:9a The greatest peacemakers are those who work for peace between God and mankind—through Jesus Christ; and those who help keep peace between brothers and sisters in Christ.

5:10a This would include taking a firm stand for what you know is right, no matter who nor how many make up the opposition.

5:10b For each of these positive statements of Christ, a counterpart is also true. In this

cute you and say all kinds of things about
you which are not true, because you are
faithfully obeying Me and talking to others
about Me.[a]
12 Always rejoice and be extremely glad when
such persecution comes, because your
reward in heaven will be great![a] Because
that's the way the prophets who lived and
witnessed faithfully for God before your
time were treated.[b]

You are to be Salt and Light

13 "You are the preserving salt with which the
people of this world are to be salted and saved.
But if the salt in your life and testimony has lost
its sharp penetrating qualities and healing pow-
ers, and has become lifeless and useless, how
will others be convinced, convicted, saved,
and preserved in purity, uprightness, and self
control by your influence and help? Such salt
is no longer good for any purpose. In fact, all
that remains then is that it be thrown out and
trampled underfoot by people because of its
worthless condition.[a]
14 "You are also to shine and give light to
everyone in the world.[a] It's impossible for
people not to see a city on a hill.[b]
15 "Neither do people light a lamp, and then
cover it with a large basket. No, they put it on
a lampstand, and then it gives light to everyone
in the house.
16 "So let your light shine before others so
they will see the good life you are living. Your
Father in heaven will receive honor when you
do that.[a]

Regarding the Law

17 "Don't think that I have come to do away
with the Law of Moses or the pronouncements
of the prophets. I have not come to do away
with them but to satisfy the Law and fulfill the
prophecies of the prophets.
18 "I tell you the absolute truth, that as long as
the heavens and the earth last, there's no possibility whatever that the smallest letter or the
smallest part of a single letter will be abolished
from the Law until its whole purpose has been
accomplished.
19 "So if you refuse to obey even one of the
least important of these commands, and teach
others that they may do so, you will be
despised by those in the Kingdom of heaven.[a]
But if you obey them, and teach others to obey
them, you will be called great by those in the
Kingdom of heaven.
20 "Because I tell you, that unless you obey
and serve God in a far better way than the
Pharisees and the teachers of the Law of
Moses,[a] there's no way whatever that you will
gain entrance into the Kingdom of heaven.

---

case, those who avoid persecution, by saying or doing what some person or the crowd wants done or said, instead of what God wants, *will not inherit the Kingdom of God*! If the positive is true, the negative is also true. This applies to the preceding verses as well.

5:11a To *faithfully obey Christ, and talk to others about Him* means to live and serve as He would if He were now in your place. 1 John 2:6. It means to think, plan, act, live, speak out, teach, warn, encourage, love, pray, and witness to others as He would if He were where you are. Expect persecution when you go all out for Him in all things. Some persecution will be subtle, some not so subtle. Matthew 13:21; 2 Timothy 3:12. If people persecuted Him they will persecute you. But consider the great results, as mentioned in the next verse. Always keep that in mind! Always!

5:12a The rewards promised in heaven will so far outweigh the temporary value of any earthly loss, that there is just no way of comparing the two values. That's the reason for the extreme happiness to be experienced in such loss. The rewards will be great! See 1 Corinthians 2:9. No doubt, the greater the dedication, and the greater the loss of worldly success and acceptance, the greater the reward.

It is recorded in Luke 6:22-23 that Christ told those who were persecuted for their faithfulness to *leap for joy* when they were persecuted for their faithful and outspoken testimony. The great reward that is assured by Christ is the reason for the extreme happiness to be expressed at such a time—and in all future time as they continue faithful.

5:12b Do lukewarm "Christians" and unbelievers speak well of you? If so, read Appendix 200.

5:13a Mark 9:50; Luke 14:34-35. And consider Romans 10:9-10 here.

5:14a ... *so people may see their true condition, and where they are going, and be guided to the way that leads to everlasting life*.

5:14b So be visible in the stand you take for Christ, and the witness you give for Him.

5:14-16a See 2nd note for Revelation 1:20.

5:19a This is not referring to your future position in the Kingdom of heaven, but as to how those presently in the Kingdom of heaven will view you (especially Christ and the Father). Because according to the next verse, such people won't even make it into the Kingdom of heaven.

5:20a Exodus 19:1 to 31:18.

Murder and Anger

21 "You have heard that it was said to our people of long ago, 'You shall not commit murder,'[a] and that whoever does must be brought to trial.
22 "But I tell you that anyone who is even angry with his brother or sister for no good reason will be in danger of being brought to trial. And whoever calls his brother or sister 'worthless,' 'stupid,' or 'shallow-brained' shall answer to the court. Anyone who says 'You worthless fool!' will be in danger of the fire of hell.
23 "So if you bring your gift to the altar, and while there remember that someone carries a grudge against you,
24 leave your gift at the altar. Go and get things straightened out with that person. Then come back and offer your gift.
25 "Come to a quick agreement with the one who is suing you, before you come to court,[a] so that he doesn't bring you before the judge, and the judge then turn you over to the bailiff to be thrown into jail.
26 "I assure you that there's no way you will get out of there until you have paid the last cent you owe.[a]

Adultery

27 "You have heard that it was said to our people of long ago, 'You shall not commit adultery.'[a]
28 "But I tell you that whoever gazes at a woman with lustful desire to sin with her has already committed adultery with her in his heart.
29 "So even if it's your best eye that's causing you to keep on sinning, gouge it out and throw it away. Because it's better that one part of your body be destroyed, than for your whole body to be thrown into hell.
30 "And if it's your right hand that's causing you to keep on sinning, then cut it off and throw it away. Because it's better that one part of your body be destroyed, than for your whole body to be thrown into hell.

Divorce

31 "It has also been said, 'Anyone who divorces his wife must give her a certificate of divorce.'[a]
32 "But I tell you that whoever divorces his wife for any reason other than marital unfaithfulness[a] causes her to commit adultery. And whoever marries a woman[b] divorced for marital unfaithfulness is committing adultery.

Jesus Forbids Oaths

33 "You have also heard that it was said to our people of long ago, 'You shall not break the oath of your promises, but you must do whatever you promised the Lord.'
34 "But I tell you, don't swear by anything when you make a promise: Not by heaven, because heaven is God's throne,
35 or by the earth, because the earth is His footstool, or by Jerusalem, because that's the city of the great King.
36 "Don't even swear by your own head, because you can't make even one hair white or black.
37 "Just say 'Yes' or 'No.' Anything more is from the evil one.

About Revenge and Giving

38 "You have heard that the Law of Moses says,

> 'If someone destroys the eye of another, he must pay by having his own eye destroyed. If one knocks out the tooth of another, his own tooth must be knocked out.'[a]

39 "But I tell you: Don't resist an evil person. If someone strikes you on the right cheek, turn the other to him also.
40 "If someone wants to take you to court and sue you for your shirt, let him have your coat as well.
41 "If someone forces you to go a mile, go two

5:21a Exodus 20:13. Jesus elevated the Law from an external act to the internal motives of the heart.

5:25a Or *while you are both still alive*. The passion you have not turned away from, the wrong you have not made right, will meet you as your adversary at the judgment bar of God.

5:25-26a A good way to take this very prudent advice from the Lord is this: You are a sinner; God has a lawsuit against you. There's only one breath between you and death. Now is the time to come to an agreement with God. You are invited to make amends with God by turning from your rebellion against Him to obeying Him, and trusting in Jesus as your Savior. Accept His invitation at once, and He will save your soul. Don't delay! Eternity is much nearer than you think. If you die in your sins you will never live where God lives. Read The Amazing Story of God, Appendix 245.

5:27a Exodus 20:14.

5:31a Deuteronomy 24:1.

5:32a Literally *fornication*.

5:32b This all applies to a man as well. See 19:9 for clearer explanation.

5:38a Exodus 21:24; Leviticus 24:20;

miles with him.
42 "Give to the one who asks you for something; and if someone asks to borrow something from you, lend it to him.

Love Your Enemies

43 "You have heard that it's been said, 'You shall love your friend,[a] and hate your enemy.'
44 "But I tell you: Make it your practice to love your enemies. Speak kindly to those who curse you, and do good to those who hate you. Pray for those who treat you with contempt and persecute you.
45 If you do this, you will be true children of your Father in heaven. Because He causes His sun to rise on evil people as well as on those who are good. And He sends rain for those who do right and for those who do wrong.
46 "What reward can you expect from God if you love only those who love you? Even people with the lowest of morals[a] do that.
47 "And if you are friendly and considerate only toward your friends and relatives, what are you doing more than others? Even the lowest criminals[a] do that.
48 "So you must always aim at conducting yourselves as fully developed followers of Mine in every situation, striving to act as perfectly and maturely as your Father in heaven.[a]

Give Honorably and Profitably

6 "Take warning: Be careful not to do your good deeds publicly, to call attention to what you've done.[a] If you do, you will get no reward from your Father in heaven.
2 "So when you give to the needy, don't broadcast the fact with trumpets, as the hypocrites do in the synagogues and out on the streets, in order to win the praise of others. I tell you the truth: They have received all the reward they will ever get.
3 "But when you give to the needy, do it in such a way that even your closest friends won't know about it, so that your giving is done in secret.
4 "Then your Father, who continually watches you[a] in secret, will Himself reward you openly.[b]

The Model Prayer

5 "And when you pray don't be like the hypocrites, who love to stand in the synagogues and on the street corners so everyone will see them. I tell you the truth: They have already received all the reward they will ever get.
6 "But when you pray, go to your room and shut the door. Then pray to your Father who is watching in secret, and your Father, who sees you there,[a] will reward you openly.
7 "And as you pray, don't keep mindlessly repeating the same words over and over again[a] like the heathen do. They think that the more words they say, the more likely they are to have their prayers heard.
8 "Don't be like them. Because your Father knows all about the things you need before you even ask Him.
9 "Instead, pray like this:
'Our Father who is in heaven, may Your name be most highly revered!
10 Reign as King in every life! May You be fully obeyed here on earth, just as You are in heaven.
11 Continue to give us the food we need for each day.
12 And forgive us all the wrongs we have

Deuteronomy 19:21.

5:43a Leviticus 19:18.

5:46-47a Literally *tax collectors*. Israel was a captive nation at this time, paying taxes to Rome. Jews who were willing to collect these taxes and get their cut were thoroughly despised by other Jews. They were also hated "sinners" because they would often charge more tax than directed, and pocket the surplus.

5:48a See 2 Corinthians 7:1, and note.

6:1a It may seem that Christ is contradicting what He said in 5:16, but this is not the case. In 5:16 Christ is challenging His followers to live in such a way that they will bring honor to God. But here in 6:1 the Lord is warning about giving to the needs of others in such a way that you seek honor for yourself. We should be careful not to desire to be recognized and praised for the help we give others in any way. Our great desire should be to serve the Lord in such a way that we will have eternal rewards. Those rewards will be of far greater value than any reward we could receive now. So live your life in such a way that you will bring honor to God (5:16), but don't seek to do anything in such a way that you will bring honor to yourself.

6:4a 2 Chronicles 16:9; Proverbs 5:21, 15:3.

6:4b God gives many rewards in this life. See Proverbs 19:17. But this likely refers to the rewards given at the great Judgment Seat of Christ. 2 Corinthians 5:10. These eternal rewards will be much greater, and obviously far more enduring, than any rewards received in this life.

6:6a ... *even though you don't see Him* ...

6:7a Praying the same words *when they*

done, in the same way that we forgive
those who have wronged us.
13 Keep us from being tempted in any way to
do wrong. Instead, liberate us from the
temptations of the flesh[a] and of the Evil
One. Because we belong to Your
Kingdom!
And all power and glory are Yours forever! May it always be so!'
14 "Because if you forgive those who have
wronged you, your Father in heaven will also
forgive you.
15 "But if you don't forgive others, neither will
your Father forgive you.[a]

True and Effective Fasting

16 "Also, when you fast,[a] don't go around with
a sad face like the hypocrites do. They actually
neglect their hair, face, and clothes, to make
sure everyone will know they are fasting. I
assure you, they already have all the reward
they will ever get.
17 "But when you fast, wash your face and
comb your hair, so that others won't know you
are fasting. Only your Father will know.
18 And your Father who is watching all that is
done, though unseen by anyone, will reward
you openly.

Make Eternal Investments in Heaven

19 "Stop piling up valuable material things for
yourselves here on earth, where every imagin-
able kind of moth and corrosion can destroy
them, and where thieves[a] can break in and
steal them from you.
20 "Instead, pile up investments for yourselves
in heaven. No disasters of any kind can
destroy them there, and no thieves can break
in and steal them.
21 "Because where your investments are,
that's where your heart will be also.[a]
22 "Your eyes act as windows for your body.
If they are clear and in good condition, your
whole body will be flooded with light.
23 "But if your eyes have degenerated and are
now useless, your whole body will be full of
darkness. In the same way, if the eyes of your
understanding, which should be giving you light
in your soul, are keeping you in darkness
instead, consider how dreadful that darkness is.[a]
24 "You cannot serve two masters. Because
either you will hate one of them and love the
other, or you will serve one with zeal and have
little or no time for the other. You cannot be
zealously occupied in serving both God and
money.[a]

Never Worry

25 "For this reason I most earnestly tell you:
Don't worry about what will be available for
you to eat and drink in order to stay alive. And
don't worry about your body, about the clothing you will need. Isn't life itself a far greater
wonder than food? And what a wonder the
body is,[a] much more so than the clothing you
put on it!
26 "Look at the birds in the air. They don't
plant seeds or gather in a harvest and put it into
barns; but your Father in heaven is continually
feeding them. Are you not much more highly
valued by God than the birds?
27 "Which of you by worry and anxious care
can add eighteen inches[a] to your height[b]?
28 "So why do you worry about clothes?
Look at the lilies out in the field, how they
grow. They don't work or make clothes for
themselves.
29 But I tell you that even Solomon, with all
the wealth and power he had, was never able

---

come from the heart is not mindless repetition. Our Lord repeated the same words three times when He prayed in Gethsemane. It's the *empty repetition* of prayers that our Lord condemns.

6:13a James 1:12-15.

6:15a See 18:23-35.

6:16a ... *going without food as part of your earnest prayer* ...

6:19a ... *of every kind* ...

6:19-21a For a very important note here, see Luke 16:9.

6:23a If the eyes of your soul are debased and are keeping you mainly concerned about earthly satisfactions and attainments—if they are diseased and are not being truly fixed on heaven and the endless eternity that stretches forever before us—how dreadful that darkness is. Jesus then goes on to apply it in the next verses.

6:24a There's nothing wrong with money and wealth that is used in a right way for the blessing of mankind and the glory of God. But wealth is treacherous, very treacherous. See Matthew 19:16-26; Mark 10:17-27; Luke 12:16-34; 16:1-13; 1 Timothy 6:10, and notes.

6:25a If God gave us the great miracles of life and a body, can't we trust Him to supply our necessary food and clothing in some way?

6:27a Literally *a cubit*—between 18 and 22 inches.

6:27b The Greek word used here can refer either to the *length of one's life* or to one's *stature*. We believe that the correct transla-

to dress himself as beautifully as one of these
flowers.
30 "Now then, if God so beautifully dresses
the grass of the field, which is here today and
thrown on the fire tomorrow, won't He even
more surely provide your clothing? How can
you have so little faith!
31 "So don't worry, saying, 'Will we have anything to eat?' or 'Will there be something to
drink?' or 'How will we get clothes to wear?'
32 "Those are the very things the people of the
world are always so concerned about. But
your Father in heaven knows all about your
need for all these things.
33 "Your chief concern, above all else, must be
to seek the Kingdom of God,[a] and to do all that
is pleasing to Him. If you sincerely do that, in
one way or another all the things you need will
be provided for you.
34 "So don't worry about tomorrow, because
with tomorrow will come the ability and the
opportunities to deal with tomorrow's problems. Today's problems are enough for you to
be concerned about today.

Stop Judging Others

7 "Stop condemning others, and God
won't condemn you.
2 "Because God will treat you in the same
way that you treat others. The same measuring
stick you use to measure others will be used by
God to measure you.
3 "And why do you fret about the tiny speck
of sawdust in your brother's eye, when, look,
you completely ignore the big log in your own
eye?
4 "How can you dare say to your brother,
'Let me take that speck out of your eye,' when
you refuse to deal with the big log in your own
eye?
5 "You hypocrite! First remove the log from
your own eye. Then you'll be able to see clearly to remove the speck from your brother's
eye.
6 "Don't give that which is sacred to the
dogs, or throw your pearls in front of the pigs.[a]
If you do, they may merely trample them
under foot, and then turn on you and tear you
to pieces.

To Pray Effectively

7 "When you pray you must earnestly persist
in your asking[a]; then what you are asking for
will definitely[b] be given you. Keep on diligently seeking,[a] and you definitely[b] will find what
you are looking for. Keep on loudly
knocking,[a] and the door will open for you.
8 "Because everyone who keeps on asking,[a]

---

tion in this case is *stature*. One could hardly know whether or not he had added any time to his life; but he would know if he had added height. In Luke 12:25-26 Jesus calls this addition of stature *of little importance*. He wouldn't likely say that about prolonging life, but it certainly is true about adding a cubit to one's height. Scientific experiments have revealed that people who exercise vigorously three times a week live longer than those who don't. So one can add years to one's life, but not several inches to one's height.

6:33a This refers to both God's Kingdom in your heart (Luke 17:21) and to His Kingdom in heaven and on earth. To *seek God's Kingdom* above everything else means that God's Kingdom everywhere, and especially in heaven, becomes your greatest and all-consuming concern. To seek that Kingdom means 1) to acknowledge your need for God's forgiveness through Jesus the Savior, 2) to live now to please God in everything you think, do, and say, and 3) to become interested and active in those exploits and pursuits that will please and glorify God. This certainly includes obeying the last command of Jesus (28:18-20) so that God may reign as King in every heart. Luke 17:21. To seek to really know God and His will must be the main business of every Christian. It is when you make God's concern for the lost your concern, that Christ promises that God will supply all your needs in this life. Philippians 4:13-19.

7:6a The meaning is, don't waste much time with people who are savage and snarling haters of the Great News. Use your time wisely, and seek those who are willing to listen. Do witness to those who oppose you, but if you encounter continued strong opposition, just say to the person, "I will leave you now to your fate, because of what Jesus said about you in Matthew 7:6." Don't quote it to them. Just walk away. Hopefully they will become so curious they will look it up, and become convicted.

But very, very few are hostile to the Great News when it's presented in love, and when you speak to them one on one. The great majority of the unconverted are more willing to listen to the Great News than most Christians are willing to speak to them about it! But are we really converted to Christ if we refuse to obey Christ and speak to others about Him? Consider Romans 10:9-10 here.

7:7,8,11a All are present tense in the Greek, representing present continuous

is definitely[b] in the process of receiving, and
everyone who keeps on seeking,[a] is definitely[b]
in the process of finding, and for the one who
keeps on knocking,[a] the door will open.[c]
9 "Would any of you men here give a stone
to your children if they asked you for bread?[a]
10 "Or if they asked for a fish, would you give
them a snake? Of course not!
11 "If you, then, evil as you are, know how to
give good gifts to your children, how much
more will your Father in heaven give good
things to those who earnestly persevere in asking[a] Him for them!
12 "In every situation treat others in the same
way that you want them to treat you. This is
the very heart of the Law of Moses and the
books of the Prophets.

The Narrow and Wide Gates

13 "You must find and enter the narrow gate in
order to get onto the road that leads to eternal
life! The gate that leads to hell and destruction
is wide, and the road leading there is broad,
and most everyone is traveling that easy road.[a]
14 "The reason so many travel the broad road
is because of the narrowness of the gate one
must enter to get onto the road that leads to
life, and because the road that leads to life is
also narrow and difficult.[a] So there are few
who are looking for it with enough diligence to
find it.[b]

Beware of False Teachers

15 "You must constantly be on the alert[a] for
men who preach a false message. They come
to you looking like gentle sheep, but if you
could look inside their hearts you would discover that they are bloodthirsty wolves who
will tear you apart!
16 "You will be able to tell what they really are
by the fruits[a] they bear. Do you gather grapes
from thorn bushes, or figs from thistles?
17 "The obvious truth is: Every good tree
always produces good fruit, but a bad tree
always produces poisonous or worthless fruit.
18 "A good tree cannot produce poisonous or
worthless fruit, and a corrupt tree cannot produce good fruit.
19 "Every tree that fails to produce good fruit
will soon be cut down and thrown into the

---

action. See Luke 11:5-13; 18:1-8.

7:7-8b All are indicative mood, the mood of certainty. See important Luke 11:9-10 note.

7:8c See important notes for Luke 17:6; John 14:13-14.

7:9a Pita bread in the Middle East is still baked in the shape of a round stone.

7:11a Present tense, representing continuous action. See Luke 11:5-13, 18:1-8

7:13a We are all on a journey. As soon as children reach the age of accountability they find themselves on the broad road, unless by that early age they have been led to accept Christ as both Lord and Savior. Romans 3:23.

There's great liberty on the broad road. You can do anything and you're still on the road. There's popularity, appearance of ease and enjoyment, hilarity (since anything goes), and jolly companionship.

But there are many disillusionment's. Only a few get rich or famous. Most of those who do are discontented, miserable, disappointed and dissatisfied. The same applies to most of the others on this road. *The way of the unfaithful is hard.* Proverbs 13:15; Galatians 6:7-8.

The way gets wider as you feed your appetites as you wish. These appetites eventually become insatiable.

There's lots of company on this road. There are the atheists, agnostics, nonreligionists, the unconverted, people of pleasure, people of "progress", every age, rank, employment—and nominal Christians. These "Christians" believe in God and Christ with their minds, but not with their hearts. They have little interest in fellowship with God in prayer, in Bible reading, in witnessing to others, or obeying all of Christ's commands. They do many good things, but they fail to realize that God considers their selective obedience as rebellion. See vss 21-27.

There's one great disadvantage to traveling this road. It leads to destruction—to the fires of an awful hell! Psalm 9:17; Revelation 20:11-15. No mere human warns of this; it's the warning of Jesus Christ. Matthew 10:28; Luke 16:19-31. If you are satisfied with the disappointing side effects caused by living this way, and the destruction and endless, excruciating, racking pain and suffering at the end of the road, continue on. But if you want real life, look for the narrow gate that leads to eternal life through Jesus Christ as both Lord and Savior.

Read Appendix 245, entitled, The Amazing Story of God. There you will discover your destiny—who you really are, what you can be, and how to reach heaven, for sure.

7:14a "In other words, the whole course is as difficult as the first step."—*Jamieson, Fausett, and Brown*. See Luke 13:24.

7:14b Are all who consider themselves Christians on the narrow road that leads to heaven? See Appendix 200A.

7:15a Present tense.

fire.[a]
20 "So you will be sure to recognize false
preachers by the fruits[a] they produce.
21 "Not everyone who continues to call Me
'Lord' will enter the Kingdom of heaven. Only
those who practice obedience to My Father in
heaven will be allowed in.[a]
22 "On Judgment Day there will be many who
will say to Me, 'But Lord! O Lord! Didn't we
prophesy and preach in Your name? We even
drove out demons and performed many miracles in Your name!'
23 "Then I will reply, 'I never knew you. Get
out of My presence, you who insist on living as
you please instead of obeying God!'[a]

Wise and Foolish People

24 "Therefore everyone who is listening to
what I have just said, and continues to put My
words into practice, is like a wise man who
built his house on the rock.
25 "The rain came down in torrents, and the
flood waters rose. The winds blew fiercely and
pounded the house, but it didn't break apart
because it was built on the rock.[a]
26 "But everyone who hears what I have just
said, and still ignores Me and fails to put My
words into practice, is like a man who was
foolish enough to build his house on sand.
27 "The rain came down in torrents, the flood
waters rose, the winds blew fiercely, pounding
the house, and it collapsed, with devastating
results."[a]
28 When Jesus finished talking, the people
who had heard Him couldn't get over the way
He had taught.
29 Because He didn't teach at all like the
teachers of the Law of Moses, uncertainly, but
with great authority.

The Healing of the Leper

8 After Jesus came down from the hillside,
great crowds followed Him.
2 Suddenly a man suffering with leprosy
came and kneeled down in front of Him, pleading, "Sir, I know that if You want to, You are
able to make me well."
3 Jesus reached out His hand and touched
him, and said, "I do want to. Be well!"
Immediately the man's leprosy was gone!
4 "Make sure you don't tell anyone about
this," Jesus told him. "But go to the priest and
show him that you are now well. Bring an
offering, as Moses instructed,[a] as a testimony
to everyone that you are healed."

A Servant Healed

5 When Jesus arrived in Capernaum, a
Roman army captain came to Him with an
urgent request.
6 "Sir," he said, "my servant is lying at home
paralyzed, and in frightful pain."
7 "I will go and heal him," Jesus replied.
8 "Sir," the captain responded, "I'm not worthy to have you come into my home. Just give
the command, and my servant will be healed.
9 "Because I have officers who give orders to
me, and I have soldiers who take orders from
me. I command, 'Go' to one, and he goes. To
another I say, 'Come' and he comes. I tell my
servant, 'Do this,' and he does it."
10 Jesus was so amazed when He heard this,
that He said to those following Him, "I tell you
the truth, I haven't found such great faith anywhere, not even among the Jews.
11 "Many[a] will come from the east and the
west, I tell you, and will sit down with
Abraham, Isaac and Jacob at the Feast in the
Kingdom of heaven.
12 "While many who should have been in the

7:19a John 15:1-6.

7:16,20a This is plural in both vss because we are not only to judge the life of the preacher, but we are to judge the results of his preaching in the lives of his listeners. Have they become doers of God's Word as a result of his preaching, or merely listeners? James 1:21-22. Within five years the majority of a congregation will have the same views and values as its minister. Pastor, what a responsibility is yours! And what a responsibility rests on those who choose or retain a certain pastor!

7:21a We must have one goal in mind—*obedience to the King*! Otherwise we are not converted.

7:23a Just how serious is this warning? Turn to Appendix 200B.

7:24-25a This is a most important prophecy by Jesus Christ. Notice what He says about acting according to what He has taught and commanded. And James says, "Faith that doesn't result in obedience to God is dead." James 2:20. The *rock* does not refer in this instance to the sacrifice of Christ, but, rather, *to His commands*. The New Testament is filled with Jesus' commands to His followers. Notice the importance Jesus places upon our obedience to those commands.

7:26-27a To be fairly warned regarding Christ's statement here, see Appendix 200C.

8:4a Chapters 13 and 14 of Leviticus.

8:11a ... *like this man* ...

Kingdom will be thrown into the outer darkness, where there will be weeping and gnashing of teeth."[a]
13 Then Jesus said to the Roman captain, "Be on your way, because what you believed for has already happened." And his servant was healed that very moment.

Many People Healed by Jesus

14 When Jesus arrived at Peter's house, He found Peter's mother-in-law sick in bed with a fever.
15 He simply touched her hand and the fever left her, and she got right up and started preparing a meal for them.
16 When evening came, the people brought many to Him who were demon possessed. He drove the evil spirits out with a single word, and He healed all who were sick.
17 In doing this He made the prophecy of Isaiah come true that says:

"He Himself took our sicknesses and carried away our diseases."[a]

The Cost of Following Jesus

18 *Sometime later,*[a] when Jesus saw the great crowds around Him, He ordered the Twelve to prepare to cross to the other side of the lake.
19 A teacher of the Law then came up to Him and said, "Teacher, I'll follow You wherever You go."
20 "Foxes have holes and birds of the air have nests," Jesus replied, "but the Son of Man has no home or possessions here, not even a pillow He can call His own."
21 Then another of His followers said, "Sir, let me stay at home until I bury my father."
22 "Follow Me," Jesus responded, "and let those who are spiritually dead bury their own dead!"[a]

Jesus Calms a Storm

23 Then Jesus and His followers got into the boat and started across the lake.
24 Suddenly, when they were part way across, a fierce storm swept down over the lake, creating such extreme turbulence that the waves towered over the boat and threatened to bury them. But Jesus just lie there sleeping.
25 So His followers rushed over to Him and shook Him awake, shouting, "Lord, save us! We're about to die!"
26 "Oh what little faith you have!" Jesus
replied. "Why are you so afraid?" Then He stood up and ordered the wind and the waves to stop their violence, and everything became completely calm.
27 The men were utterly amazed. "What kind of man is this!" they exclaimed. "Why, even the wind and waves obey Him."

Two Men with Demons Healed

28 When they arrived at the other side of the lake, in the district of the Gergesene people, two demon-possessed men came out from among the tombs in a graveyard and met Him. They were extremely fierce, so much so that no one dared to travel the road there.
29 Suddenly they screamed, "What business do you have in coming to us, Jesus, you Son of God? Have you come to torment us before the appointed time?"
30 Not far from them was a large herd of pigs feeding.
31 "If You force us out," the demons pleaded, "please allow us to enter that herd of pigs."
32 All Jesus said was, "Go!" And they came out of the men and promptly entered the herd of pigs. But immediately that whole herd of pigs ran violently down a steep bank and into the lake, and drowned.
33 When that happened, the men herding the pigs ran into town and reported everything that had happened, including what had happened to the demon-possessed men.
34 And look! Everyone in town was coming out to angrily confront and threaten Jesus. But once they saw Him they merely begged Him to leave their part of the country.

Jesus Heals a Paralyzed Man

9 So Jesus got into the boat and crossed back over to the town where He lived.
2 Soon after, some men came to Him bringing a man who was paralyzed, lying on a stretcher. Seeing how strong and determined their faith was,[a] Jesus said to the paralytic, "Cheer up, My son. Your sins are forgiven."
3 Immediately some of the teachers of the Law thought to themselves, "This man's a blasphemer[a]!"
4 But Jesus knew what they were thinking, so He said, "Why are you thinking such evil thoughts?
5 "Which is easier to say, 'Your sins are forgiven,' or, 'Get up and walk'?

8:12a See Mark 9:44-48 note.
8:17a Isaiah 53:4.
8:18a Implied, from Mark 4:35.
8:22a This man wanted to follow Jesus, but wanted to wait until his father had died, which could be many years later. Christ wanted this man to know that following and serving Him was of far more importance than any other obligation.
9:2a Mark 2:3-12.
9:3a *"...Who does he think he is? Only God can forgive sins!"* Mark 2:7; Luke 5:21.

6 "But so that you may know that the Son of Man has authority on earth to forgive sins...'Stand up!' He said to the man. 'Now fold up your stretcher and be on your way home.'"

7 And he got right up and went home!

8 When the crowd saw this, they were astounded, and praised God for giving such power to men.

The Calling of Matthew

9 As Jesus went on from there, He saw a man named Matthew sitting in the tax collector's booth. "Come with Me," Jesus invited him. And Matthew got right up and went with Him.

10 Matthew then invited Jesus and His followers to his home for dinner. He also invited many other tax collectors[a] and other sinners.

11 When the Pharisees saw this, they asked His followers, "Why does your teacher eat with these crooked tax collectors[a] and other sinners!"

12 Upon hearing this, Jesus said, "Healthy people don't need a doctor, but sick people do.

13 "But go and learn what this Scripture means: *'I am even more concerned that you be merciful to others, than that you sacrifice to Me.'*[a] I didn't come to call those who consider themselves so godly that they have no need of further help. I'm here to call sinners to turn from their sinning to living lives of obedience to God."

A Question about Fasting

14 One day the followers of John the Baptizer came to Jesus and asked Him, "Why is it that we and the Pharisees often go without food, but Your followers never fast?"

15 "Would you expect the guests at a wedding reception to go without food while the bridegroom is with them?" Jesus asked in reply. "But the time will come when the bridegroom will be taken from them. They will indeed fast then.

16 "No one sews a piece of unshrunk cloth onto an old garment, because when the patch would shrink it would pull away from the old cloth and make a bigger hole.

17 "Nor does anyone pour new wine into old wineskins. Because the wine would swell and burst the old skins. Then the wine would spill out, and the skins would also be ruined. New wine is put into new wineskins; then both are preserved."

One Dead and One Sick

18 While He was still speaking to them, an official of the synagogue rushed up and knelt before Him, saying, "My daughter has just died! But come and put Your hand on her, and she will live again."

19 So Jesus and His followers got up and went with him.

20 Then with extreme urgency, a woman who had suffered a severe bleeding problem for twelve years came up behind Him and touched one of the tassels of His prayer shawl.

21 "If I can just touch His shawl," she had said to herself, "I will be healed."

22 Jesus turned around, and looking at her He said, "Take courage, My daughter, your faith has made you well." And the woman was instantly healed!

23 When Jesus entered the official's home and saw the funeral musicians and the wailing crowd,

24 He said, "Everybody out! The girl is not dead, but asleep." The people there couldn't believe anyone would say such a thing at such a time, and they laughed at Him in scorn.

25 But when the crowd had been put out, He went into the girl's room and took her by the hand, and the girl got right up!

26 News about this great miracle spread throughout all that part of Israel.

Two Blind and One Mute Healed

27 As Jesus left there, two blind men began following Him and shouting, "Son of David! Have pity on us!"

28 When He went indoors, the blind men went in too. So Jesus asked them, "Do you believe I am able to do what you are asking?"

"Yes, Sir, we do!" they replied.

29 So He touched their eyes, and said, "Let it happen then, as you believe."

30 Immediately they could see! "Now listen:" Jesus strongly ordered them, "Do not tell anyone about this."[a]

31 But when they left, they told everyone about Him throughout that whole region.

32 And as these men were leaving the house, a man was brought to Jesus who was demon-possessed and couldn't talk.

33 After Jesus forced the demon out, the man started talking! The crowd was amazed, saying, "Nothing like this has ever happened before in Israel!"

34 But the Pharisees said, "It's the ruler of the demons who gives him the power to drive out demons."

A Bumper Harvest—Pray for Workers!

35 Jesus traveled through all the cities and towns, teaching in their synagogues, telling the Great News about the Kingdom of God,

---

9:10-11a See 5:46-47 note.
9:13a Hosea 6:6. See also 1 Samuel 15:1-23.

9:30a For the reason see 12:16 note.

and healing every kind of disease and sickness of the people.

36 When He saw the crowds, His heart went out to them, because they were weary and helpless, like sheep without a shepherd.

37 "There are so many people to harvest," He said to His followers, "but so few workers to harvest them.

38 "So plead most earnestly[a] with the Lord of the harvest so that He may use His great power in forcibly thrusting out[b] laborers into His great harvest field."

10 Then Jesus called together His twelve followers. He gave them power to drive out evil spirits and to cure every kind of disease and sickness.

2 The names of the twelve apostles[a] were: Simon, better known as Peter; his brother Andrew; James, the son of Zebedee; his brother John;

3 Philip; Bartholomew; Thomas; Matthew, the tax collector; James, the son of Alphaeus; Lebbaeus, whose last name was Thaddaeus;

4 Simon, the Canaanite; and Judas Iscariot, the one who betrayed Him.

Apostles Instructed and Sent Out

5 Jesus sent these twelve out with the following instructions: "Do not go to the Gentiles,[a] and don't go into any Samaritan[b] towns.

6 "Instead, go to the lost sheep of Israel.

7 "As you go, cry out to the people, 'The Kingdom of heaven has come very near to you!'

8 "Heal the sick, cure the lepers, restore the dead to life, and drive out the demons. What you received was given you free of charge; now give without expecting to be paid.

9 "Don't bring gold, silver, or money of any kind with you.

10 Don't carry a knapsack[a] or an extra coat or shoes or walking stick; because the worker is worthy of being supported by those to whom he ministers.[b]

11 "When you come to a city or town, ask the people there who they would recommend as an upright and worthy person, and stay in his home until you leave.

12 "And when you go to a home, greet the people there warmly.

13 "If they offer you their support and cooperation, ask God's blessing on them. But if they offer no help, keep the blessing you had reserved for them.

14 "And when you leave the house or city where the people refuse to receive you or listen to your message,[a] shake the very dust of that place from your feet![b]

15 "I tell you the truth, God will show more mercy to the people of Sodom and Gomorrah on Judgment Day than to the people of that city or home.

Beware of Trouble

16 "Now listen! I am sending you out as sheep among wolves. So be as cautious as snakes and as harmless as doves.

17 "You must constantly be on your guard against certain people. Because they will have you arrested, tried in their religious courts, and whipped in their synagogues.

18 "And because you represent Me, you will be brought before governors and kings, so that you can tell them and their people about Me.

19 "But when they arrest you, don't worry about what you should say at your trial, or how you should say it, because the words will be given you when it's your time to speak.

20 "It won't be you speaking, but the Spirit of your Father in heaven will be speaking through you.

21 A man will even betray his brother and have him put to death. Fathers will betray their own children, and children will turn against

---

9:38a The Greek word here means *beg, plead, implore*—not merely *ask*. This harvest is a matter of life or death, forever!

9:38b Actual meaning of the Greek word. "The verb *ekballō* really means to drive out, to push out, to draw out with violence or without." *A.T. Robertson*, in *Word Pictures in the New Testament*.

10:2a One who is sent as a messenger.

10:5a All who are not Jews.

10:5b Samaritans were a mixed blood, only part Jewish. 2 Kings 17:24.

10:10a ...*for food and other essentials* ...

10:9-10b The Lord wanted them to experience how well He could supply all their needs as they served Him, if they would only have faith in God to meet their needs. Take care not to spend your life making provision for self-support before obeying the call of God. Later (see Luke 10:4; 22:35-36) Jesus instructed His workers to bring along and use anything in their possession that could be used in their support, even a sword for defensive purposes.

10:14a It was possible that not one home in an entire town would open to them.

10:14b By this symbolic action they would vividly separate themselves from all connection with those who were rejecting the Lord, severing themselves from all guilt or respon-

their parents and have them put to death.
22 "You will be hated by everyone because of
the stand you take for Me.[a] But if you remain
faithful to Me to the end of life you will be
saved.[b]
23 "When they persecute you in one city,
move on quickly to the next, because I tell you
the truth, you won't even cover all the cities in
Israel before the Son of Man comes.[a]
24 "A student can't expect to be treated with
greater respect than his teacher; nor a servant,
than his master.
25 "So a student should be satisfied if he is
treated in the same way that his teacher is, and
a servant, in the same way that his master is. If
they have called Me, the Master of the house,
Beelzebul,[a] it is certain they will call the members
of My household even worse names.

Fear only God

26 "But don't be afraid of them. Because
there's nothing that's now covered up that

---

sibility for that rejection.

10:22a The early Christians were very bold in their stand for Christ. They spoke out and reached the then-known world with the message of the Savior. According to the apostle Paul, the same is necessary for Christians today if we are to be saved. See v 39 and note, and Romans 10:9-10. Can you truthfully say you love God if you refuse to obey Christ (28:18-20) and open your mouth to speak out for Him, and warn those who are lost of their awful condition, and point them to your Lord and Savior?

Read what God told John would happen to cowards. Revelation 21:8. And God is saying the same to every Christian today that He said to Ezekiel (Ezekiel 33:8-9), when He said, *When I say to the wicked, 'O wicked man, you will surely die', and you don't speak out and do your best to persuade him to change his ways, that wicked person will die because of his sin, but I will hold you responsible for what will happen to that lost person because of your neglect and unwillingness to obey Me and speak to him. But if you do warn that wicked man to turn from his evil ways, but he still doesn't do so, he will die lost because of his sin, but you have saved your own soul.*

It's time that those who claim to be Christians take the bold stand for Christ that God demands. When we wake up to the seriousness of our responsibilities, God will bring the great spiritual awakening that is so desperately needed. For help in your witnessing read the notes on Matthew 28:18-20 and appendixes 212, 226, and 245.

But be warned: When the church really goes on the offensive as God demands, you can expect to be hated and persecuted even as the early church was. But we will also see the same results that they saw. We are living in the end of the age, and we don't have long years ahead of us to do the work for Christ that needs to be done. We must work while we still have the opportunity. The harvest is ripe and ready to be brought in! Always remember that Romans 10:9-10 is just as relevant to your salvation as John 3:16. God is deeply concerned that you be deeply concerned about the welfare and salvation of others, to the same extent that you are concerned about the salvation of your own soul. See 22:39. Jesus was willing at awful cost to be your Savior, and now He expects you to expend yourself and be the savior of others! Otherwise your claim to being converted to Him is a hollow claim. And when you witness to others be sure to let them know that being converted to Christ includes going public for Him.

For far too long the Christian world has been given the false impression that speaking out for their Lord was optional. That's a lie from Satan! Eternal life, or judgment by God, are at stake! You can easily begin a witness for Christ with anyone by simply asking them, "Are you planning on making it to heaven?" Their answer to the question will tell you what to say next. You can ask that question of anyone, at any time, at any place. You can even go up to a perfect stranger and begin a witness for Christ by asking that question. Even if they walk away you have at least planted a seed in their heart and mind.

Jesus said, "If you are ashamed of Me among the sex-crazed and sinful people of your time, ashamed to fly your colors and share with others the message of Life that I came from heaven to earth to give lost mankind, I, the Son of Man will also be ashamed of you when I come in the glory of My Father with the holy angels." Mark 8:38. What will be the destiny of those who are ashamed of Christ and are unwilling to take a stand and speak out for Him? See appendix 209.

10:22b Revelation 2:26.

10:23a *...to judge Israel.* Which happened when Rome crushed Israel only 40 years later, in A.D. 70.

10:25a Beelzebub (lord of flies) was a god of the Ekronites. 2 Kings 1:2. In derision the Jews changed one letter in the word and gave the name to Satan in an Aramean form—Beelzebul (god of dung, or filth). By giving the name to Christ, they poured upon Him the greatest possible abuse and con-

won't one day be uncovered; and nothing hidden that won't then be exposed.
27 "Whatever I tell you in the dark, speak it
out in broad daylight; and what I whisper in
your ear, preach it from the housetops[a]!
28 "Never be afraid of people. The most they
can do is kill your body, but they can't kill your
soul. But always fear God, who is able to bring
both body and soul to utter ruin in hell!
29 "Don't they sell two sparrows for a mere
copper coin? Still, not one of them falls to the
ground without your Father knowing about it
and allowing it.
30 "But as for you, God even knows the number of hairs on your head.
31 "So don't be afraid, because you are of far
more value to God than an enormous number
of sparrows.[a]

Never be Ashamed of Jesus

32 "So if you will speak out and tell others
how much I mean to you,[a] I will tell My Father
in heaven that you belong to Me.
33 "But if you ignore or disown Me when with
others[a]—I will also disown you before My
Father in heaven.[b]

Jesus' Declaration of War and His Call to Arms!

34 "Don't get the idea that I have come to
bring peace to the earth. I have not come to
bring peace, but war!
35 "Because My coming, and the message I
bring, will turn sons against their fathers,
daughters against their mothers, and daughters-
in-law against their mothers-in-law.
36 "Your worst enemies will many times be the
members of your own family.[a]
37 "If you love your father or mother, or son
or daughter more than you love Me, you are
not qualified to be a follower of Mine!
38 "Neither are you qualified to bear My name
if you are unwilling to take up your cross[a] and
follow Me, in My steps.[b]
39 "If you insist on living your life as you yourself please, you will lose it, but if you will lose
your present life for My sake, you will find it in
eternal life.[a]

---

tempt.

10:27a Freely and fearlessly tell others all that God has taught you. Leave the consequence with God.

10:31a God created you to be one of His children. And through Christ He has made it possible for you to be forgiven your rebellion and sin and be restored to His family. He has such great plans for you.

10:32a A confession of Christ includes our actions as well as our words. We are therefore to confess Christ in every circumstance of life and before everyone. It is not merely in *one* act that we are to do it, but in every act, taking advantage of every opportunity to speak out for the Lord, and to take a stand for Him. Again, see Romans 10:9-10.

10:33a Christ can be disowned by both words and actions, and by silence, in refusing or neglecting to speak out and act according to His many commands in the New Testament. Obedience refused is to deny or disown Christ as Lord. To be born again means that we have turned from our rebellion to God, and we now obey the Lord. Without obedience (holiness) a person will never see God. Matthew 7:21-23; Romans 6:22; 10:9-10; Hebrews 12:14. When either heaven or hell are at stake, silence is treason!

10:33b Mark 8:38.

10:36a When you in truth *take your stand* for Christ and for what He taught, you will be declaring your opposition to the lost world's standard. And the opposition you will face as a result can be very brutal.

10:38a The cross Christ is speaking of here is not sickness, suffering, trials, disappointment, or adversity of any other kind. A cross is an instrument of death! Christ calls *all* of His followers to death—to willingly die to all selfish desire and ambitions, and work industriously to further His Kingdom and glory and our future glory. Proverbs 3:35; Romans 5:2; 8:18; I Corinthians 15:43. See Appendix 221.

10:38b Christ died for you. He now asks you to die to yourself for His sake and for the sake of others who need life. He asks for your affection—unto death! Are we worthy of His love and sacrifice for us if we give Him anything less? To carry our cross and follow Him means to do our full duty toward God and man, no matter what others may think, say, or do.

10:39a Christ is actually saying, "Anyone who is mainly concerned about 'having it made' in this life, with his comfort, security, and pleasures here, and who denies Me by avoiding any rejection he might experience by openly confessing to one and all that he loves Me and lives only to please Me (Romans 10:9-10), will lose eternal life. But the one who lives only to please Me, and is willing to lose out in much, or all, that this brief life offers as he gives his life to Me, will gain eternal life."

We are not saved by works, it is true. But it is also true that we are not saved unless we are truly born again, resulting in our hav-

Promised Rewards

40 "The person who welcomes you is welcoming Me, and the one who welcomes Me is actually welcoming the One who sent Me.
41 "When you welcome and help someone who is faithfully and boldly speaking out for God, because you recognize him as a true messenger of God, you will receive the same reward that he will. And when you welcome and assist a good man because of the fact that he is living to please God, you will receive the same reward that he will.
42 "And if you give as little as a cup of cold water to one of the least admired followers of Mine, because of the fact that he is My follower, I tell you the truth, you won't fail to be rewarded, even for that."

Messengers from John the Baptizer

11 When Jesus had finished instructing His twelve followers, He left there to teach and preach in the neighboring cities.
2 While in jail, John heard about the things the Messiah[a] was doing, and he sent two of His followers to Him.
3 "Are you the One[a] we were promised would come?" they asked Him. "Or are we to keep on looking for someone else?"
4 "Go back and tell John what you've been hearing and seeing," Jesus replied.
5 "People who were blind now see, those who were lame are walking, lepers have been cured, the deaf can hear, the dead are being brought back to life, and the Great News is being preached to the poor.
6 "Happy and blessed by God is the person to whom I will not be a stumbling block."
7 As John's followers were leaving, Jesus said to the crowds concerning John, "What kind of person did you go out into the wilderness to see? Were you looking for someone who resembled a stock of tall grass that is easily swayed this way or that by whichever way the wind is blowing[a]?
8 "But what kind of person did you actually go out to see? Were you looking for a man dressed in expensive clothes? No, those who wear fine clothes live in expensive homes.
9 "But why did you go out? To see a prophet? Yes, I tell you, and you found one who is far greater than any other prophet.
10 "Because John is the one about whom God was speaking when He said to His Son:

> 'Listen! I am sending My messenger to go ahead of You. He will prepare the people to receive You.'[a]

11 "I tell you the truth, no woman has ever given birth to anyone who has risen to a higher level of greatness than John the Baptizer. But even the least important person in the Kingdom of Heaven is greater than John is now.
12 "And from the days that John the Baptizer started preaching, until now, the Kingdom of Heaven has been under siege, but only those who are thoroughly and fiercely determined to enter are gaining entrance.[a]
13 "Because all the pronouncements of the Law of Moses and of the prophets[a] before John looked forward to this time.
14 "And if you are willing to receive it, John is Elijah,[a] who is yet to come.
15 "If you have been given ears for the purpose of hearing, then give serious consideration to this.
16 "But to what can I compare the response of you people of today? The situation is similar to children sitting in the marketplaces, whose

---

ing the sincere desire and intention of doing all that is required of us by our Lord, according to His instructions in Scripture. That all this refers to eternal life, and not merely eternal rewards, see Mark 8:34-38 and the notes there.

11:2a *Messiah* is the Hebrew, and *Christ* the Greek translation.

11:3a Deuteronomy 18:15,18; Isaiah 7:14; 9:6-7; Jeremiah 23:5-6; Micah 5:2; Zechariah 9:9.

11:7a Meaning *someone who is swayed by every person's opinion or criticism*. See Luke 7:24 note.

11:10a Malachi 3:1.

11:12a "Our Lord is describing the energy with which some people are pressing in, and urging the need of such energy if salvation is to be obtained."—*A. Lukyn Williams. in Pulpit Commentary*.

"He that will *take*, or get possession of the kingdom of righteousness, peace, and spiritual joy, must be in earnest: All hell will oppose him in every step he takes; and if a man be not absolutely determined to give up his sins and evil companions, and have his soul saved at all hazards, and at every expense, he will surely perish everlastingly. This requires a *violent* earnestness."—*Adam Clarke Commentary* See Luke 13:24.

11:13a They were the instructors concerning the Messiah who was to come, until John came.

11:14a Very likely meaning, John is *like* Elijah, because even John said he was not Elijah. John 1:21. He came in the spirit of Elijah. Luke 1:17. Elijah will return shortly before God judges the earth *before the com*

playmates call out to them and complain,
[17] 'We played wedding music for you on the flute, but you wouldn't dance! We sang funeral songs, but you wouldn't cry!'
[18] "Because when John came he didn't eat or drink with others, and they said, 'He has a demon in him.'
[19] "On the other hand, the Son of Man came eating and drinking with anyone and everyone, and they say, 'Look at him! He's nothing but a gluttonous drunkard, and a friend of tax collectors and other sinners!' But wise actions are always later proved to be right by the results."

Disaster Awaits Unrepentant People

[20] Then He began to publicly denounce the people in the cities where most of His miracles had been performed, because they hadn't turned from their sinning to living to please God.
[21] "Awful misery and suffering lies ahead for you people in Chorazin! The same awaits you in Bethsaida! Because if the great miracles I performed in your cities had been performed long ago in sinful Tyre and Sidon, those people would have turned from their sinning and obeyed God. And to show their sorrow for their past sins they would have dressed in rough sackcloth and put ashes on their heads.
[22] "I assure you, the people of ancient Tyre and Sidon will receive a lighter sentence on Judgment Day than you will!
[23] "And you people of Capernaum, you who have been lifted up to heaven,[a] you will be delivered down into hell! Because if the great miracles I performed in your city had been performed in Sodom, it would have remained a city to this day.
[24] "And I tell you, those who lived in Sodom will receive a lighter sentence on Judgment Day than you will."

There is Rest for the Weary

[25] Then, in reference to what He had just said, Jesus prayed, "O Father, Lord of heaven and earth, I thank You for hiding these things from those who consider themselves to be so wise and learned, and revealing them instead to those who are childlike in faith and acceptance.
[26] "Yes, My Father, because that's the way You were pleased that it should be."
[27] Then turning to His followers He said, "My Father has delivered everything into My hands. And no one really knows the son—only the Father does. And no one really knows the Father, except the Son, and those to whom the Son chooses to reveal Him.[a]
[28] "Come to Me, all of you who labor and are burdened down with so many cares, and I will give you rest.
[29] "Accept My direction for your life and learn from Me, because I am gentle and humble in heart, and you will find rest for your souls.
[30] "Because My yoke[a] is easy to wear, and the load I ask you to carry is actually light."

A Question about the Sabbath

12 Around that time Jesus was walking by some grainfields on a Sabbath day.[a] His followers were hungry, so they began breaking off some heads of wheat and eating the kernels.
[2] When the Pharisees saw this they said, "Look, your followers are harvesting grain on the Sabbath! That's unlawful!"
[3] "Haven't you ever read," Jesus replied, "what David did when he and his men were hungry?
[4] "He went right into the house[a] of God and ate the sacred bread, which was not lawful for him or his men to eat. Only the priests were allowed to eat it.

---

ing of the great and dreadful Day of the Lord. Malachi 4:5-6.

John was not Elijah reincarnated. Nowhere does the Bible teach reincarnation. Hebrews 9:27 states, "It has been determined by God that men are to die only once. After that they must stand before Him for judgment." If Enoch and Elijah are the two witnesses of Revelation 11:3-13, they will not be reincarnated, because neither of them has died yet. Genesis 5:18-24; 2 Kings 2:1-11.

In the Passover seder (service) today Jews still put a place setting on the table for the Prophet Elijah. The final segment of the seder is called the "cup of Elijah" looking forward to the coming of Elijah as the forerunner of Messiah.

11:23a Jesus had made Capernaum His headquarters during His entire public life. It was the most favored spot on earth, the most exalted in privilege. Today, some of God's greatest witnessing is being done in the USA. As in Capernaum, God is offering you heaven—unless you are satisfied to continue on to hell. Romans 3:23; 6:23.

11:27a The Son will reveal the Father to all who give clear evidence of true and total desire to make Him Lord of all their life.

11:30a A *yoke* is a wooden frame to fasten two animals together to pull a load, a plow, etc.

12:1a Saturday, the Jewish day of rest.

12:4a That is, the tabernacle tent. The

5 "Or haven't you read in the Law of Moses that on the Sabbath days the priests work in the temple, actually breaking the Sabbath law, but are not judged guilty?

6 "But I'm telling you that One far greater than the temple is with you now.

7 "And if you had known the meaning of the Scripture, *'I am even more concerned that you show kindness to others, than that you sacrifice to Me,'*[a] you would not have condemned the innocent.

8 "Because I, the Son of Man, am even the Lord of the Sabbath."

Jesus Heals on the Sabbath

9 After leaving there Jesus went into their synagogue, where He saw a man with a withered hand.

10 Looking for a way to bring a charge against Jesus, some men asked Him, "Is it lawful to heal on the Sabbath?"

11 "If one of your sheep fell into a pit on a Sabbath," He replied, "which of you men wouldn't grab hold of that sheep and lift it out?

12 "Consider then how extremely valuable a man is compared with a sheep! Of course it's lawful to do good on the Sabbath!"

13 "Stretch out your hand," He then said to the man. So he stretched it out, and it was restored, just as full of life and vigor as the other!

14 But the Pharisees went out and plotted together as to how they might destroy Him.

Jesus, God's Chosen Servant

15 Knowing this, Jesus withdrew from there. But still, great crowds followed Him, and He healed all who were sick.

16 But He strongly ordered them not to tell anyone what He had done for them.[a]

17 All this happened so that what God had said through Isaiah the prophet would come true, when He said:

18 "Look! Here is My Servant whom I have chosen. I love Him dearly, and have found such great delight in Him. I will put My Spirit upon Him, and He will alert people everywhere of their duty toward their God and the consequences of disobedience.

19 He will not argue or shout, and no one will hear Him preaching loudly in the streets.

20 He will not break off a reed that is bruised.[a] And He will not snuff out a faintly burning flame,[b] until He has caused justice to triumph.

21 People throughout the nations will put their hope in Him."[a]

Jesus and Beelzebul

22 Then some people brought a man to Jesus who was blind and couldn't talk because he was demon-possessed. And Jesus healed him, so that he could both see and speak.

23 That entire great crowd was amazed, and exclaimed, "This Man couldn't be the Messiah, could He?"

24 But when the Pharisees heard that statement, they said, "The only reason he's able to drive out the demons is because he's doing it with power given him by Beelzebul,[a] the ruler of the demons."

25 Jesus knew what they were thinking, and He told them, "Any country that's divided, with one side fighting another, is in the process of being destroyed. Any city or family that allows

---

temple hadn't yet been built.

12:7a Hosea 6:6.

12:16a Too much public acclaim would only increase the fury of the opposition, causing them to demand His death immediately, before His work was finished.

God had chosen the time and place for Him to die. He was the Lamb of God (Exodus 12:1-14; 29:38-39; Isaiah 53:7; John 1:29,36; 1 Peter 1:19; Revelation 5:6; 12:11) who must die in Jerusalem on the day of Passover as God's sacrifice for the sins of the world. The Passover Lamb was killed at twilight (right after sundown, which was the beginning of the day in Israel), on the 14th day of the first Jewish month, Nisan. Leviticus 23:5. Christ was sacrificed on the same day at nine o'clock in the morning (Mark 15:25), as the 14th of Nisan began at the previous sundown. And He died at three in the afternoon of the same day.

So the last Jewish Passover recognized by God was observed during the first 12 hours of the 14th of Nisan. After which, God made His sacrifice (during the last 12 hours of the same day) for the sins of all the world.

When this happened this was God's New Testament, or God's New Agreement with mankind, regarding the forgiveness of our sins. John 3:16.

12:20a He will not break the person who is weeping and mourning and broken in spirit because of sin; that is, He will not be severe, unforgiving, and cruel. He will pardon, heal, and give strength.

12:20b He will not further oppress those who have little strength. He will not extinguish life and hope when it seems to be almost gone.

12:21a Isaiah 42:1-4.

12:24a See 10:25 note.

internal fighting won't last either.

26 "So if Satan allows part of his forces to war against his other forces, he's fighting himself. How long could his kingdom continue under such conditions?

27 "If I'm driving out demons with power given Me by Beelzebul, by whom do your own followers drive them out? So even they will refute and cut the ground out from under your claim.

28 "But if I'm driving out demons by the power of the Spirit of God, that proves that the Kingdom of God has arrived among you.

29 "Or look at it this way: How can a man enter a strong man's house and take what he has, unless he first ties up the strong man? Then he can take whatever he wants.[a]

30 "Anyone who is not working with Me is working against Me.[a] And everyone who is not gathering souls with Me is actually chasing them from Me.[b]

31 "That's why I tell you, people can be forgiven any sin and any evil thing they say, but anyone who says anything evil against the Holy Spirit will not be forgiven.

32 "If you speak evil against the Son of Man, you can be forgiven, but anyone who speaks evil against the Holy Spirit will not be forgiven—not in this age or in the age to come.

Two Kinds of Fruit

33 "If you want good fruit, you must plant a tree of a good variety; if you plant a tree of a poor variety, you won't be able to eat the fruit. The kind and variety of a tree is known by the fruit it bears.

34 "You children of snakes! How can you, filled as you are with evil, say anything good? Because whatever fills a man's heart comes out in what he says.

35 "From the good treasures in a good man's heart come good things, and from what an evil man treasures in his heart come evil things.

36 "I'm warning you, that on Judgment Day everyone must give an account of every worthless word they have ever spoken.

37 "Because by the words you have spoken you will either be declared free from guilt, or you will be condemned."

The Demand for Proof

38 Then some of the Pharisees and teachers of the Law said, "Teacher, we want you to show us a miraculous sign."[a]

39 You're asking for another sign," He replied, "because you're part of an evil and adulterous generation that refuses to believe Me. But no further sign will be given you except the sign that will resemble what happened to the prophet Jonah.

40 "Because just as Jonah was inside a great fish for three days and three nights, so will the Son of Man be in the heart of the earth for three days and three nights.[a]

41 "The people of Nineveh[a] will rise from their graves on Judgment Day at the same time you do, and condemn you, because they turned from their sinning to obey God when Jonah preached to them.[a] And the truth is, One who is far greater than Jonah is speaking to you now!

42 "The Queen of the South[a] will also rise from her grave on Judgment Day when you do, and she will condemn you as well, because she came a long way to listen to the wisdom of Solomon. The truth is, One who is far greater than Solomon is here now![b]

An Evil Spirit Will Return, Unless God is Invited in and Obeyed

43 "When an evil spirit goes out of a person, it looks in the desert for a place to rest.

44 "When it doesn't find any it says to itself, 'I'll go back to the home I left.' When it returns, it finds the place empty, clean, and everything in order.

12:29a Jesus is the one who can tie up Satan's demons.

12:30a There is no middle ground.

12:30b There can be no neutrality concerning Christ. You are either truly for Him and working with Him, or you are against Him, and your indifference or opposition gives evidence of it. To fail to openly take a definite stand for Christ, and openly defend His truths and His true servants, is to be a deserter and a traitor. Romans 10:9-10.

12:38a Previously, these men had claimed that Jesus' power came from Satan. Now they're asking for further proof that His power is from God. Luke 11:16 records that they asked for *a sign from heaven*. They wanted Him to cause something to happen in the heavens. But He had given sufficient proof already. Even today, people still doubt the great sign He promised in the next verses that He would give. See vss 39-40. Later on, in Matthew 16:1, some Pharisees again ask for a sign from heaven.

12:40a ... *Then He will rise back to life again.*

12:41a Jonah 3:1-10.

12:42a I Kings 10:1-13.

12:42b ... *and you refuse to listen to Him and believe Him.*

45 "Then it goes off and gets seven other spirits more evil than itself, and they all come and
live there. As a result the person is now worse
off than he was before. And the same thing
will happen to you people who continue to
live in sin today!"

The True Family of Jesus

46 While He was still speaking to the crowds,
His mother and brothers came and stood outside the packed house, asking to speak to Him.
47 "Sir," someone said, "Your mother and
brothers are standing outside, wanting to talk
to You."
48 "Who is My mother?" He replied. "And
who are My brothers?"
49 Then stretching out His hand toward His
followers, He said, "Here are My mother and
My brothers!
50 "Because whoever does what My Father in
heaven wants him to do is My brother, sister,
and mother."[a]

A Story about a Farmer

13 That same day after Jesus left the house,
He went down to the lake and sat down.
2 But such great crowds came to Him there,
that He soon got into a boat and sat in it out on
the lake, while the people stood on the shore.
3 Then He talked to them about many things,
using parables to illustrate what He was saying.
"Once there was a farmer," He said, "who
went out to plant seed.
4 "As he scattered the seed, some fell on the
hard path alongside the plowed field, and the
birds flew down and ate it.
5 "Some fell on rocky areas where there was
little soil. The stalks came up quickly because
the soil was shallow and warm.
6 "But when the sun rose higher they were
scorched, because they weren't able to put
their roots down. So they withered away.
7 "Some fell among thistles, and the thistles
sprang up and choked the plants.
8 "But some seed fell into good soil, and pro-
duced a crop that was a hundred, sixty, or thirty times what had been sown.
9 "Let the one who has been given ears with
which to hear, seriously consider what I've
said."

The Purpose of Parables

10 Some of His followers then asked Him,
"Why do you speak to the people in parables?"
11 "Because you have been given the privilege
of understanding the secrets of the Kingdom of
Heaven," He replied, "but it has not been
given to them.
12 "Because whoever is continuing to highly
esteem and preserve what he is receiving from
Me,[a] will be given more, and he will end up
with great understanding. But whoever does
not highly esteem what he's receiving,[a] even
the little he now has will be taken from him.
13 "That's the reason I use these illustrations—
because although they can see, most of them
are not looking with any real interest. And
although they can hear, they aren't really listening, nor do they make any real attempt to
understand.
14 "These people fulfill the prophecy of
Isaiah, through whom God said:

> 'When it comes to hearing, you will keep
> on listening, but you won't really under-
> stand; and when it comes to seeing, you
> will keep on looking, but you won't really
> grasp the truth.
> 15 Because the heart-center of the deep emo-
> tions of these people has become flabby.
> So it's hard for them to listen to what's
> being said, and they've closed their eyes. If
> they hadn't allowed themselves to get into
> such a deplorable spiritual and moral condi-
> tion they would be able to see with their
> eyes and hear with their ears and under-
> stand with their hearts. Then they could be
> changed in their thinking and in their ways,
> and I, the Lord, would heal them.'[a]

16 "But how fortunate you are, because your
eyes are taking in what there is to see, and your

12:50a As dear and tender as the ties were that bound Him to His mother, brothers, and sisters, those that bound Him to His true followers (those who obeyed His Father) were even more tender and sacred. How great is His love for His followers, when it is even greater than that for His mother! And what a brilliant illustration of His own teaching, that we must forsake father, mother, and friends, and houses and lands to be His followers.

Though many of Christ's followers are poor, despised, and unknown by the rich and famous, they are more dear to Him than mother, sisters, and brothers. So cheer up if you are a faithful follower of Christ. You are loved by the greatest One of all, and by His Father, who is Lord of all.

13:12a The present tense in this context is a present continuing action. And the subject under consideration is knowledge, wisdom and understanding of spiritual truth. Mark 4:25; Luke 8:18; 19:26.

13:15a Isaiah 6:9-10.

ears are intently listening to what I say.

17 "I tell you the truth, many prophets and good men of the past had great longing to see what you are now seeing, but they didn't see it, and to hear what you are now hearing, but they didn't hear it.

The Meaning of the Parable

18 "So listen now to the meaning of the parable about the farmer:

19 "When someone hears the message about the Kingdom of God, but has little real interest in understanding it, Satan comes along and snatches away the words that were planted in his hard heart. That was illustrated by the seed that fell on the hard path alongside the plowed field.

20 "The rocky areas that received the seed represent the one who, upon hearing the message, immediately and joyfully accepts it.

21 "But he doesn't allow the teaching to go deep into his life, so the message and its effect last for only a short while. When he's given a hard time and is persecuted because of his faith in the message, he quickly gives up and falls away.

22 "Now the thistle area that received the seed represents the one who gladly understands and accepts the message, but because of his divided interest, in being anxiously concerned about his earthly problems and the deceitful glamour of money, the great message is choked. He comes to the place at last where he isn't bearing any fruit.[a]

23 "But the one who earnestly listens to, and also reads God's message for himself with an honest and open heart, who then understands and accepts its demands, restricting conditions, and promised great blessings and rewards is like the good soil that received the seed. He then shares his testimony and what he has learned with others, and brings thirty, sixty, and even a hundred or more into God's Kingdom.[a]

About Wheat and Weeds

24 Then Jesus gave them another parable: "The Kingdom of Heaven is also like what happened when a man sowed good seed in his field.

25 "One night when everyone was asleep, his enemy came and sowed weeds[a] in the field where the wheat had been sown, and then left.

26 "When the wheat grew and formed heads of grain, then one could see the heads of the weeds too.

27 "The farmer's hired men then went to him and said, 'Sir, didn't you sow good seed in your field? Then where did all these weeds come from?'

28 'An enemy did this!' he exclaimed.

'Shall we go out then and pull up the weeds?' his men asked him.

29 'No,' he said, 'you'd be in danger of uprooting the wheat at the same time.

30 'Let them both grow together until harvest time. Then I'll tell the harvesters to first gather the weeds and tie them in bundles to be burned, and then bring the wheat into my barn.'"

A Mustard Seed and Yeast

31 Then He told them another parable: "The Kingdom of Heaven is also like what happens when a man plants a mustard seed[a] in his field.

32 "It's the smallest seed of all, but when it's grown, it's larger than any other plant, and becomes a tree, so that the birds of the air come and perch in its branches."

33 Then He gave them still another parable: "The Kingdom of Heaven is like yeast, which a woman mixed into a large bowl of flour, causing the whole batch of dough to rise."

34 Jesus illustrated everything He said to the crowd that day with a parable. He didn't say anything to them without using a parable.

35 In doing this He fulfilled what the prophet declared, when he said:

> "I will open My mouth and speak in parables, revealing things that have been kept secret since the world was created."[a]

A Parable Explained

36 Then Jesus sent the crowds away and went into a house. His followers then came to Him and said, "Please tell us what You meant in the parable about weeds in the wheat field."

37 "I, the Son of Man, am the One planting the good seed," He replied.

38 "The field is the world, the good seeds are the people who belong to the Kingdom of

---

13:22a See John 15:1-6, and the note for Luke 8:14, to discover what happens to those who don't bear fruit.

13:23a Where do you fit into this parable? See Appendix 205.

13:25a Actually *darnel*, a weed resembling wheat. This is a good illustration of cults. They resemble the real thing but are not.

13:31a This is evidently the black mustard, *Brassica nigra*. The seed is the size of a fleck of ground pepper, and the plant may grow to a height of fifteen feet. It is still common in Israel.

13:35a Psalm 78:2.

God, the weed seeds are Satan's followers.
39 "The enemy who planted weeds among the
wheat is the devil. The harvest is the end of
the age, and the harvesters are the angels.
40 "Just as the weeds are to be gathered up
and burned, that's what will happen at the end
of the age.
41 "The Son of Man will send out His angels
to sort out of His Kingdom all persons who
tempt others to sin, and all who practice sin.
42 "Then they will throw them into the blazing
furnace, where they will weep and wail in
awful anguish and regret, and gnash their teeth
in pain.[a]
43 "Then those who have lived pure and hon-
orable lives will shine as brilliantly as the sun
in the Kingdom of their Father. Let those who
have been given ears for the purpose of hearing, listen!

Buried Treasure

44 "Also, the Kingdom of Heaven is like a treasure that a man found hidden in a field. He hid
the treasure again, and was so ecstatic about it
that he sold everything he had and bought the
field.[a]
45 "The Kingdom of Heaven is also like a mer-
chant looking for beautiful pearls.
46 "When he found one that was extremely
valuable, he went out and sold everything he
had, and bought it.[a]

Like Sorting Fish

47 "Also, the Kingdom of Heaven is like a
dragnet thrown into the lake, which caught
every kind of fish.
48 "When it was full the fishermen pulled the
net ashore. Then they sat down and sorted the
good fish into containers, and threw the bad
ones out.
49 "That's how it will be at the end of the age.
The angels will sort out those who lived sinful
lives from those who lived to please God,
50 and will throw the sinful ones into the blazing furnace, where they will weep and wail in
awful anguish and regret, and gnash their teeth
in pain.
51 "Do you understand all of this now?" Jesus
asked.

"Yes, Lord," they said. "We do."
52 "Very well," Jesus continued. "Because
you say you understand, let Me say this: Every
person who has been instructed in the things of
the Kingdom of Heaven to the point where he
understands the truth, is like the owner of a
home who is able to bring out both antique
and new furniture from his storeroom."[a]

Jesus Rebuffed in His Home Town

53 When Jesus finished giving these parables,
He left the area.
54 When He came to Nazareth, His hometown, and began to teach in their synagogue,
the people were astonished. "Where did he
get all this wisdom?" they asked. "And the ability to do these miracles?
55 "Isn't this the carpenter's son? Isn't Mary
His mother? And aren't James, Joseph, Simon,
and Judas His brothers?
56 "Don't all His sisters live here in our town?
Where then did He get all this?"
57 And they deeply resented Him. But Jesus
told them, "A prophet isn't without honor,
except in his hometown and among his own
family members."

13:40-42a Matthew 25:41; Luke 16:19-31; Revelation 14:9-11; 20:10-15. See Mark 9:44,46,48 note.

13:44a The Kingdom of heaven is indeed a great treasure! It is worth giving our all to obtain! It's only our selfishness and the wrongful pampering of our various appetites that are keeping us from that eternal treasure of everlasting life there. And we can only obtain it by accepting God's forgiveness through Jesus Christ, and making a full surrender of our lives to Him as Lord. Do it! Failure to do so will mean no eternal treasure of eternal life in heaven to look forward to—only the Great Judgment, for sure. Don't delay! Satan wants you to put it off until later, and then later, and then... Don't wait! Satan's game is fixed. You can't win with him. Open your heart to Jesus now! You have no promise of a sure tomorrow, only the present moment is yours. Do it !

13:46a Here the Kingdom of heaven is likened to the most beautiful and most valuable gem that one can find. We should gladly be willing to sacrifice all other things to obtain it. Even the *anticipation of eternal life with God* is a joy and immense pleasure each day.

13:52a In ministering to others they were now to use truth from both the Old Testament and from the new truth He was giving them. When you have come to understand the truth, you are then able to teach others, by bringing out the truth from both the Old and New Testaments, from old and new experiences in life (both spiritual and physical), from old truths to be rediscovered and from new truths yet to be discovered in God's Word.

58 So He didn't do many miracles there because of their unbelief.

John the Baptizer Beheaded

14 It was at this time that Herod, the ruler of Galilee, heard the news about Jesus.

2 "That's John the Baptizer!" Herod told his attendants. "He's come back to life again, and that's why He has power to do these miracles!"

3 Because he was living in adultery with Herodias, his brother Philip's wife, Herod had earlier ordered John's arrest, and had him chained in jail,

4 because John had kept telling him, "You are breaking God's Law[a] by living with your brother's wife!"

5 Herod had wanted to put him to death, but he was afraid the people would mob him if he did, because they considered John a prophet.

6 But when they celebrated Herod's birthday, the daughter of Herodias danced for those at the party.

7 And Herod was so immensely pleased that he promised with an oath to give her whatever she wanted.

8 After being pressured by her mother, she said, "I want the head of John the Baptizer right here, on a platter."

9 The king was greatly distressed that she'd made that request, but because of the oath he had made in front of all his dinner guests, he ordered John's head to be given her.

10 So he sent someone to behead John in jail.

11 The head was then brought on a platter and given to the girl, who brought it to her mother.

12 Afterward John's followers came and took his body and buried it, and then went and told Jesus what had happened.

Jesus Feeds 5,000 People

13 Upon hearing of John's death, Jesus immediately went by boat to a deserted area to be alone. But when the crowds heard He was leaving, they left the towns and followed Him on foot.

14 When Jesus got out of the boat and saw the huge crowd, His heart was filled with pity for them, and He healed the sick among them.

15 As evening was approaching, His followers went to Him and said, "This is a deserted area, and it's getting late. You'd better send these crowds away, so they can go into the towns and buy food for themselves."

16 "They don't need to leave," Jesus responded. "You give them something to eat."[a]

17 "But all we have here are five small loaves of bread[a] and two fish!" they replied.

18 "Bring them here to Me," He said.

19 Then He told the people to sit down on the grass. And taking the five loaves and two fish, He looked up to heaven and asked God to bless the food. Then He broke the loaves and gave them to His followers, who in turn gave them to the people.

20 All the people ate until they were full. And when they collected the leftovers, they filled twelve baskets![a]

21 About five thousand men had eaten, not counting women and children.

Jesus Walks on the Lake

22 Immediately after this Jesus made His followers get into the boat and go ahead of Him across the lake, while He sent the crowds away.

23 After He had dismissed the crowds, He went away by Himself into the hills to pray. When it got dark He was there alone.

24 Meanwhile the boat was being tossed about by the waves in the middle of the lake. What's more, they were rowing against the wind.

25 Sometime between three and six o'clock in the morning Jesus went out to them, walking on the lake!

26 When His followers saw Him walking toward them on the water, they were terrified. "It's a ghost!" they cried out in fear.

27 Immediately Jesus spoke to them. "Keep up your courage, men!" He said. "It is I. Don't be afraid."

28 "Lord," Peter then spoke up, "if it's really You, order me to come out to You on the water."

29 "Come," Jesus responded. And Peter climbed out of the boat and started walking on the water toward Jesus.

30 But when he noticed the big waves caused by the powerful wind, he became frightened and began to sink. "Lord, save me!" he cried out.

31 Instantly Jesus reached out His hand and caught him. "Oh what little faith you have," He said. "Why did you doubt Me?"

32 And the instant Jesus and Peter climbed into the boat, the wind stopped blowing.

14:4a Leviticus 18:6,16; 20:21.

14:16a See Mark 6:37 note.

14:17a A loaf of bread was generally seven inches in diameter, and half an inch to one inch thick.

14:20a After feeding that immense crowd they had far more food left over than when they started!

33 Then those in the boat came and bowed
down and worshiped Jesus, saying, "Truly you
are the Son of God!"
34 After crossing the lake, they landed at
Gennesaret.
35 When the people there recognized Jesus,
they spread the news of His coming throughout the whole region. Soon they were bringing
all the sick people to Him.
36 And they begged Him to let them at least
touch the fringe of His prayer shawl. And all
who did were made perfectly well!

It's what's Inside that Matters

15 Then several Pharisees and teachers of
the Law from Jerusalem came up to
Jesus.
2 "Why don't your followers obey the traditions of the elders?" they challenged Him.
"They don't even go through the hand washing
ceremony before they eat their food!"
3 "And why do you disobey God's commands in order to obey your traditions?" Jesus
replied.
4 "God has commanded, 'Honor your father
and mother.[a] Anyone who treats his father or
mother with disrespect must be put to death.'[b]
5 "But you say, 'Whoever tells his father or
mother, "Whatever financial help you might
have received from me, I have dedicated as a
future gift to God's work," is no longer allowed
to use his money or property to help his father
or mother.'[a]
6 "By doing so, you have nullified God's
commands to honor one's father and mother in
favor of your tradition[a]!
7 "You hypocrites! God spoke the truth
about you through Isaiah when He said:
8 'These people draw near to Me and honor
Me with words, but their hearts are far
from Me.
9 The worship they offer Me is worthless,
because what they teach as truth is merely
a set of rules made up by men, instead of
the laws I have given them.'[a]"
10 Then He called the crowd together and
said, "Listen! This is something you must
understand!
11 "It is not what a person puts into his mouth
that makes him unclean, but what comes out of
it—that's what pollutes his soul."
12 Following this His followers went to Him
and said, "Do You know that the Pharisees
have been greatly offended by what You've
been saying?"
13 "Every plant that My Father in heaven
didn't plant will be pulled up by the roots," was
Jesus' reply.
14 "Don't bother with them. They are blind
leaders who are leading the blind. And when a
blind person leads another who is blind, both
will fall into a pit."
15 Then Peter spoke up and said, "Please
explain what You meant by what You said
about uncleanness."
16 "Are you still as dull as the rest?" Jesus
responded.
17 "You certainly know that whatever food
you put into your mouth goes into your stom-
ach and is finally eliminated?
18 "But foul words coming from a person's
mouth come from the very heart of his being,
and that's what reveals how unfit he is to be
with God.[a]
19 "Because it's from the very central core of a
person's being that evil thoughts come that
lead to murders, adulteries, sexual immorality,
thefts, false testimony, and slander.
20 "These are the things that pollute a person
spiritually. But to eat with hands that have not
been ceremonially washed has nothing to do
with making a person unfit to be with God."

A Woman's Constant, Unrelenting Faith

21 Jesus then left there and went to an area
near the cities of Tyre and Sidon.
22 While there a Canaanite woman living in
the area pled with Jesus and persistently continued pleading, "O Lord, Son of David, have
pity on me! My daughter is demon possessed
and is suffering terribly!"
23 But Jesus completely ignored her. After
awhile, His followers went up to Him and
urged Him to do something about her, saying,
"Please send her away.[a] Her constant pleading
back there is getting to us."
24 "I haven't been sent to anyone except to
the lost sheep of Israel," Jesus replied.
25 Then the woman, herself, went right up to
Jesus and, kneeling before Him, pleaded,
"Please, sir, help me!"
26 "It's not right for Me to take the children's

15:4a Exodus 20:12; Deuteronomy 5:16.

15:4b Exodus 21:17; Leviticus 20:9.

15:5a See Mark 7:11 note. This all applies to money. But it is just as important that we show real loving care for our parents in many other ways as well. Failure to do so is known by God, and will surely bring down His wrath in judgment upon you sooner or later.

15:6a ... *in order to get their money for yourselves*!

15:8-9a Isaiah 29:13.

15:18a 12:33-37.

15:23a ... *with her cure*. This is certainly implied from Jesus' next words.

bread and throw it to the dogs,"[a] He replied.

27 "That's true, sir," she said, "but even the little dogs get to eat the crumbs that fall from their masters' table."

28 "O woman, your faith is indeed great[a]!" Jesus replied. "Your request is granted." And her daughter was instantly healed!

29 Leaving there, Jesus traveled toward Lake Galilee, where He walked up a hillside and sat down.

30 Immense crowds converged on Him there, bringing the lame, blind, dumb, disabled, and many others, and laying them down at His feet. And He healed them.

31 That huge crowd was amazed at what they both saw and heard. People who couldn't speak were now talking. Disabled people were made well and strong,those who had been lame could now walk, and the blind could see. That whole crowd rejoiced and praised the God of Israel.

Jesus Feeds 4,000 People

32 Then Jesus called His followers to Him and said, "I have deep concern for these people. They have stayed with Me now for three days, and have nothing left to eat. I don't want to send them away hungry, or some of them may collapse on their way home."

33 "But where can we ever get enough food in this wilderness to satisfy everyone in this massive crowd?" His followers responded.

34 "How many loaves of bread do you have?" Jesus asked them.

"Seven, and a few small fish," they replied.

35 So He ordered the people to sit down on the ground.

36 Then He took the seven loaves[a] and the fish, and gave thanks to God for them. Next He broke the loaves and fish into pieces, which His followers then distributed to the crowd.

37 Everyone ate until they were full! Then they gathered up seven large hamper baskets full of leftovers.

38 Four thousand men had eaten, besides women and children!

39 Then He sent the people on their way, got into a boat and went to the region of Magdala.

Another Demand for Proof

16 There the Pharisees and Sadducees came to test Jesus, asking Him to prove He was from God by causing something miraculous to happen in the sky.

2 "When the sky is red in the evening," He replied, "you say, 'It will be a beautiful day tomorrow, because the sky is red.'

3 "But when the sky is red in the morning you say, 'It will be a stormy one today, because the sky is red and threatening.' You hypocrites! You know how to interpret what the sky is revealing, but you can't interpret the signs that apply to these times!

4 "You're asking for another sign because you're part of an evil and adulterous generation that refuses to believe Me. But no further sign will be given you except the sign that will resemble what happened to the prophet Jonah."[a] Then He left them and left the area.

The Warning about Yeast

5 When they got to the other side of the lake, Jesus' followers realized they had forgotten to bring any bread with them.

6 So when Jesus warned them, "Watch out and always be on your guard against the yeast of the Pharisees and Sadducees,"

7 they discussed the matter among themselves, and concluded, "He said that because we didn't bring any bread with us."

8 Knowing what they were discussing, Jesus said, "Oh what little faith you have! Why are you worried about not bringing bread[a]?

9 "Don't you understand yet? Don't you remember the five small loaves that fed the five thousand men, and the many baskets of fragments you gathered up?

10 "Or the seven small loaves that fed four thousand men, and the many large hamper baskets of leftovers you gathered up?

11 "How is it that you don't understand that I was not talking to you about bread when I warned you to constantly be on your guard against the yeast of the Pharisees and Sadducees?"

12 Then they realized that Jesus had not been telling them to be on their guard against the yeast in bread, but to watch out for the teachings of the Pharisees and Sadducees.

Peter Confesses Jesus to be Messiah

13 When Jesus came into the region of Caesarea Philippi, He asked His followers, "What are people saying about Me? Who do they say the Son of Man is?"

15:26a The Jews considered themselves children of God. And they were accustomed to refer to all other people as *dogs*.

15:28a Jesus said she had great faith because she refused to be denied. Luke 11:5-13; 17:6; 18:1-8.

15:36a See 14:17 note.

16:4a See 12:38-41.

16:8a *...and concluding among yourselves that I'm concerned about the same thing?*

14 "Some say You're John the Baptizer," they replied. "Some say Elijah; others, Jeremiah, or one of the other prophets."

15 "What about you? Who do you say I am?"

16 Simon Peter spoke up and said, "You are the Messiah, the Son of the living God."

17 "Right you are, Simon, son of Jonah," Jesus replied. "But you didn't make up your mind about this by human reasoning. My Father in heaven favored you by revealing it to you.

18 "And I also say to you that you are Peter,[a] but it is on this solid Rock of truth[b] that I will build My Church. And the gates of hell[c] will never overpower it.[d]

19 "And I will give you the keys to the Kingdom of heaven, and whatever you may forbid on earth must be that which is already forbidden in heaven, and whatever you may permit on earth must be that which is already permitted in heaven."[a]

20 Then He gave a firm command to His followers not to tell anyone that He was the Messiah.[a]

Jesus Predicts His Death and Resurrection

21 From that time on Jesus began to tell His followers that He must go to Jerusalem and suffer in many ways at the hands of the elders, chief priests, and teachers of the Law; that He must be killed; but that three days later He would be raised back to life again.

22 On hearing this Peter took Him aside and began to rebuke Him. "God forbid!" he said. "No, Lord, such a thing must never happen to You!"

23 Turning to Peter and squarely facing him, Jesus said, "Get behind Me, Satan! You are a stumbling block to Me, because you don't see things as God sees them. You reason only from man's viewpoint!"

Take up your Cross!

24 Then Jesus said to His followers, "Whoever makes up his mind to follow Me[a] must determine to refuse to live any longer for the purpose of pleasing and satisfying his own natural

---

16:18a ... *solid as a rock* ...

16:18b The *Rock* on which Christ would and has built His Church was the affirmation that Peter had just given, that Jesus was the Messiah, the Son of God.

16:18c Ancient cities were surrounded by walls. In the entrance gateways were the principal places for holding court, transacting business, and deliberating on public matters. The meaning here is that no plots or attacks of any kind by Satan's cohorts against Christ's Church, would ever be successful in overpowering it.

16:18d Or *the gates of hell will never be able to stand against it*. Meaning, the gates of hell do not have power to stand against the powerful offensive march of Christ's triumphant Church. This is also true.

A good modern paraphrase of Christ's words here could be, *No matter how brilliantly the forces of hell conspire and plot, and powerfully attack to bring about its downfall, they will never succeed in overpowering it in its powerful forward march*. But when the work of the Church is finished, Christ will allow the Antichrist to finally overpower them. Daniel 7:20-22,25: 8:24; 11:32-35; 12:7b; Matthew 24:9; Revelation 13:7. But just when Antichrist thinks everything is going his way, Christ will return and powerfully defeat the forces of hell, and set up His eternal Kingdom.

* * *

Caesarea Philippi. The setting could hardly be more dramatic. The city was a symbol of the might and splendor of the Roman Empire, located at the foot of Mt. Hermon. Here a huge cave (regarded by the Greeks as the "Gate of Hades") opened up in the rock facing of the mountain from which flowed one of the sources of the Jordan River. Beside it was a gleaming white temple dedicated to Augustus Caesar. Up the valley from here stood a vast triad of Graeco-Roman temples dedicated to Jupiter, Dionysus, and Venus.

In this setting Christ prophesied that the Church would attack the "Gates of Hades". Indeed, within a century the Christian Great News had essentially turned "the world upside down" throughout the heathen world in spite of fierce imperial persecutions. The true Church is again pitted against demonical-energized forces in the world as the age draws to a close.

16:19a See 18:18**a** note, as the same rule of grammar applies here. Also notice that while Jesus is here speaking to Peter, He gives the same keys of the Kingdom to all of His followers in 18:18.

16:20a That is, they were not to witness to this fact at this time. See 12:16 note for the reason. The actual meaning is *that He was the expected Savior, the One anointed by God to be Lord of all*. The name Jesus means *Savior*. *Christ*, or *Messiah*, means the *anointed one*.

16:24a That is, to be a Christian.

desires.[b] Taking up his own cross,[c] he must die to those selfish and flesh-satisfying desires, and make it his practice to continually endeavor to fully obey what I have taught and commanded.[d]

25 "Because if you choose to continue to satisfy your desire to live as you yourself please, you will lose your soul! But if you will make it your definite purpose in life to put to death your own desires, and live as I desire you to live, you will save your soul.[a]

26 "Because what good would it all do you even if you gained all the wealth and power and all the flesh-fulfilling experiences in all the world,[a] but then found yourself barred from heaven and sent to your judgment in hell? Or look at it this way: If you suddenly found yourself in awful suffering in hell, how much would you then be willing to give of yourself to God in order to gain His forgiveness and eternal life[b]?

27 "Because I, the Son of Man, will soon come in the glory of My Father with His angels. I will at that time reward every person according to what he has done.[a]

28 "I tell you the truth: Some of you standing here right now will definitely not die until you have seen the Son of Man coming in His Kingdom."[a]

When Heaven Came Down

17 Six days later Jesus took Peter and the brothers James and John, and led them up a high mountain where they were alone.

2 As they were standing there, Jesus became altogether changed in appearance! His face became as brilliant as the sun, and His clothes became as dazzling white as light!

3 Then suddenly Moses and Elijah appeared, and began talking with Him.

4 Peter then spoke up and said, "Lord, it's wonderful that we can be here! If you are willing, allow us to put up three shelters—one for You, one for Moses, and one for Elijah."

5 But even as he was speaking, a bright cloud covered them completely, and a voice spoke from the cloud, saying, "This is My Son whom I love so dearly, and with whom I am so well pleased. Keep on listening to Him!"[a]

6 On hearing God speak, Jesus' followers were so terrified that they threw themselves facedown on the ground.

7 Then Jesus walked over and touched them. "Stand up," He said. "Don't be afraid."

8 When they looked up, they saw no one there but Jesus.

9 As they were coming down the mountain Jesus gave them strict orders, saying, "Don't tell anyone about the vision you've just seen until the Son of Man has risen from the dead."

16:24b See notes for Mark 8:34.

16:24c Regarding *your cross* see Appendix 221.

16:24d Literally *must follow Me.*

16:25a What does this really mean? See Appendix 206.

16:26a And you're willing to settle for so little of it, for so brief a time—that could end tonight; when all is yours for all eternity if you will turn from your rebellion and sin, and turn to God and accept His rightful lordship of your life, and His forgiveness. And when you do, remember, you will not be on your own. God will help you all the way. See Philippians 2:13.

16:26b In a full sense the Lord is actually saying: *Or look at it this way: If you die tonight, lost, and suddenly find yourself suffering awful pain and anguish in hell, how much will you then be desperately willing to give of yourself to God, and utterly die to all your sinning by refusing any longer to satisfy the wrong desires of your body and mind, and instead, sincerely worship, obey, serve, and take a firm stand for God, in order to get free from there and escape to heaven?*

But then it will be too late! In hell there will be no possible way out, even if you'd be willing to serve God as a slave for all eternity. Live for Him now! You can't be sure you'll be here tomorrow. But you do have the present moment. Today is your day to decide for God, and be saved! Then in heaven you will live for all eternity as one of God's glorified children, enjoying riches, pleasures (Psalm 16:11), and total fulfillment of such magnitude that cannot even be imagined by the present human mind. See 1 Corinthians 2:9. Act now, before it's forever too late. See extensive notes on the same statements by Christ in Mark 8:34-38.

16:27a Jesus is saying here that He is the Judge who will come. And He will judge us according to how we have obeyed His warnings and commands in verses 24-26. He will reward those who have taken these words to heart and obeyed them. He will give them glory, honor and eternal happiness in heaven. But those who have ignored His warnings and commands will be sent to hell as their reward. No plea of church membership or of service rendered can take the place of obedience to any of Christ's commands. Hebrews 5:9; 2 Peter 1:10.

16:28a See Mark 9:1 note.

17:5a We likewise must keep on listening to Him.

10 His followers then asked Him, "Why then do the teachers of the Law insist that Elijah must come before the Messiah will come?"[a]
11 "It's true," Jesus replied, "Elijah will come first. And when he comes, he will restore everything.[a]
12 "But I tell you, Elijah has already come[a] but the Jews didn't recognize him, and they treated him in whatever way they pleased. The Son of Man is about to suffer in the same way at their hands."
13 The followers then realized He was speaking about John the Baptizer.

The Healing of a Boy

14 When they came down to the crowd that was waiting, a man came up to Him and kneeling before Him most earnestly pled,
15 "Lord, have pity on my son! He's an epileptic, and suffers so frightfully from seizures that he often falls into fire or into water.
16 "I brought him to Your followers, but they couldn't heal him."
17 "O you unbelieving and hard-headed people!" Jesus reprimanded them. "How long must I be with you? How long must I put up with you? Bring the boy here to Me."
18 Jesus then sternly commanded the demon in the boy to come out, and it came out. The boy was instantly healed.
19 Later Jesus' followers went to Him when He was alone and asked Him, "Why couldn't we drive that demon out?"
20 "Because of your unbelief," Jesus replied. "I tell you the absolute truth: If you will continue to exercise[a] whatever faith you have in the same determined, persistent way that a tiny mustard seed goes to work,[b] you will say to this mountain, 'Move from here to there,' and it will move. Nothing will be impossible for you.
21 "But the only way this kind of demon can be forced out is by both prayer and fasting."
22 While they were staying in Galilee, Jesus told His followers, "The Son of Man is about to be betrayed into the hands of men who will kill Him.
23 "But three days later He will be raised back to life again." His followers were extremely sad when they heard this.[a]

Paying the Temple Tax

24 When Jesus and His followers arrived at Capernaum, those who collected the temple tax approached Peter and said, "Your Teacher does pay the temple tax, doesn't he?"
25 "Of course He does!" Peter replied.

When Peter entered the house Jesus spoke before Peter had a chance to open his mouth. "What are you thinking about, Simon?" He asked. "From whom do the kings of the earth collect customs or taxes—from their own children, or from others?"
26 "From others," Peter responded.

"Then the King's children don't have to pay," Jesus returned.
27 "But so that we don't offend them, go to the lake and throw out your fishing line. When you open the mouth of the first fish you catch you will find a coin. Take that and pay the temple tax for the two of us."

The Greatest in Heaven

18 It was at this time that Jesus' followers came to Him and asked, "Who will be the greatest in the Kingdom of heaven?"
2 In answer Jesus called a little child to Himself, and had the child stand in the middle of the group.
3 "Now I tell you the truth," He said, "unless there's a drastic change in your life, and you turn from your sinning to living in obedience to God, and take upon you the humble attitude of a little child toward God and the world,[a] there's no way that you will even gain entrance into the Kingdom of heaven.[b]
4 "So whoever humbles himself and

17:10a ... *if You are the Messiah, and Elijah is to come before You*? Malachi 4:5-6.

17:11a His ministry will be to restore people to faith in God and to obedience to Him, and to a proper understanding about the Messiah.

17:12a John the Baptizer came in the spirit of Elijah. Luke 1:17. But the Scripture is clear that Elijah will return in person shortly before God judges the earth (Malachi 4:5-6), and some believe he may be one of the two witnesses of Revelation 11:1-14. See Matthew 11:14 note.

17:20a Present tense (continuous action).

17:20b See Luke 17:6 notes.

17:23a All that registered in their minds at the time was that He would be killed.

18:3a ... *without selfish ambition, pride, or a haughty attitude*. We must regard ourselves as God regards us, as mere beginners. It cannot be degrading to think of ourselves as we really are. But haughty pride, or any attempt to be thought of as more important than we really are is foolish, wicked, and degrading.

18:3b ... *let alone being the greatest* ...

becomes the most like this little child will be
the greatest in the Kingdom of heaven.
5 "And whoever warmly welcomes a little
child like this, to do for him what I would do,[a]
is welcoming Me.

Frightful Punishment Awaits Tempters

6 "But whoever causes one of these little
ones who believe in Me to lose his faith, or to
sin, would be better off if someone had hung a
massive millstone around his neck, and had
drowned him in the bottom of the ocean![a]
7 "Woe to everyone in the world because of
all the temptations there are. These temptations are sure to come, but awful misery and
suffering lie ahead for the person who does the
tempting.
8 "So if your hand or foot causes you to sin,
cut it off and throw it away! It's far better for
you to gain eternal life maimed or crippled,
than to have two hands and two feet and be
thrown into the fire where the flames will rage
forever.
9 "And if your eye causes you to sin, gouge it
out and throw it away! It's far better for you to
gain eternal life with only one eye, than to
have both eyes and be thrown into the fires of
hell![a]
10 "You must always be most careful not to
look down on or mistreat any of these little
ones, because I warn you that their guardian
angels are continually making their reports in
heaven directly to My Father.[a]
11 "Because the Son of Man has come to save
all who have been lost.[a]

The Parable of the Lost Sheep

12 "What does a man with a hundred sheep
do if one of them wanders away? Doesn't he
leave the ninety-nine and go into the hills and
search diligently for the lost one?
13 "And if he finds it, I tell you the truth, he
will rejoice more about that sheep than about
the ninety-nine that didn't go astray.
14 "That's the way it is with your Father in
heaven. He doesn't want even one of these little ones to be lost.

If a Follower Sins Against You

15 "If a follower of Mine sins against you, talk
to him privately about the wrongdoing. If he
listens and admits his wrong, you have won
him back.
16 "But if he won't listen, go to him again and
take one or two other people with you, so that
'everything may be supported by the testimony
of two or three witnesses.'[a]
17 "If he still won't listen, bring the matter up
before the church. But if he won't even listen
to the judgment of the church, then treat him as
an unbeliever or as one who is working for the
benefit of the enemy.[a]
18 "I tell you the truth, whatever you forbid
on earth must be that which has already been
forbidden[a] in heaven, and whatever you permit on earth must be that which has already
been permitted[a] in heaven.[b]
19 "And listen! If two of you agree on earth
concerning anything you are praying for, My
Father in heaven will do it for you.
20 "Because where even two or three of you
come together as My followers, I am right
there with you."

Parable of the Unmerciful Servant

21 Then Peter asked Jesus, "Lord, how many

18:5a Literally,...child like this *in My name* ...

18:6a ... *before he had a chance to commit such a dastardly act.* This is a frightful warning for anyone who would tempt someone to sin. The *little ones* here applies especially to Christians who are children in the faith, and easily led. Pastor, Sunday School teacher, are you preaching and teaching the truth as God's Word reveals the truth, or as you want to believe it? Consider the consequences!

18:9a See Mark 9:43-48 note.

18:10a ... *telling Him how those under their guardianship are being treated.* Spiritually—*Be most careful that you don't despise anyone who has become humble and childlike in their life and attitude toward God, because their guardian angels* ...

18:11a So Jesus is deeply interested in even the very weakest, the least talented, and least desirable persons. He deeply loves even me!

18:16a Deuteronomy 19:15.

18:17a Literally *tax collector*. These were Jews who collected taxes from Jews for Rome, their conqueror.

18:18a Both of the words *forbidden* and *permitted* are in the perfect tense. "The perfect is the tense of completed action. It implies a process, but views the process as having reached its consummation and existing in a finished state. The point of completion is always that which has existed before the time implied or stated in connection with the use of the perfect."—*Dana and Manty Greek Grammar*. So our judgments must always agree with what God's Word reveals as truth.

18:18b See 16:19.

times should I forgive someone who keeps on
sinning against me? Seven times?"
22 "Not just seven times," Jesus replied, "but
seventy times seven.[a]
23 "You see, the Kingdom of heaven is like a
king who wanted to bring his accounts up to
date with his servants.
24 "He had just begun to do so when a man
was brought to him who owed him over eleven
million ounces of silver.[a]
25 "But because he was unable to pay, his
master ordered that everything he had was to
be sold, and that the man and his wife and children were to be sold into slavery to pay off the
debt.
26 "Upon hearing the sentence the servant fell
to his knees before him, frantically pleading,
'Master, be patient with me, and I will pay you
everything I owe!'
27 "The king was genuinely sorry for him, so
he released him and forgave the debt.
28 "But that same servant went out and found
one of his fellow servants who owed him one
hundred denarii.[a] He grabbed him and began
choking him, demanding, 'Pay me what you
owe me!'
29 "The man fell to his knees at his feet,
earnestly pleading, 'Be patient with me, and I
will pay you everything!'
30 "But he wouldn't listen. Instead he had
him arrested and thrown in jail until he had
paid what he owed.
31 "When his fellow servants saw this, they
were very upset and went to the king and told
him all that had happened.
32 "So the king called the first servant back in
and said, 'You detestable, worthless servant! I
forgave you that entire enormous debt because
you so earnestly pleaded with me.
33 'Shouldn't you also then have pity on your
fellow servant, just as I had pity on you?'
34 "His king was so angry that he sent him to
the torture chambers to be tortured until he
had paid all that he owed.
35 "And that is exactly what My heavenly
Father will do to you, unless each of you sincerely forgive the person who has sinned
against you."[a]

Marriage, Divorce, and Remarriage

19 When Jesus had finished speaking, He
left Galilee and went into Judea, and
then to the other side of the Jordan River.
2 Giant crowds followed Him there, too, and
He healed those who were sick.
3 The Pharisees also came, again testing Him.
"Does our Law allow a man to divorce his wife
for just any reason?" they asked Him.
4 "Haven't you read the Scripture," He
replied, "that says that the Creator, who made
people at the beginning, 'made them male and
female,'[a]
5 and then said, 'For that reason a man shall
leave his father and mother and be united to
his wife; and the two shall become so devoted
to each other that they become as one
person'[a]?
6 "So they are no longer two, but one. And
man must not separate what God has joined
together."
7 "Why then did Moses say that a man could
hand his wife a certificate of divorce and send
her away?" they demanded.
8 "Moses allowed you to divorce your
wives," Jesus replied, "because of the hardness
of your hearts.[a] But that's not the way it was
in the beginning.
9 "And I'm telling you that whoever divorces
his wife, and then marries another woman, is
committing adultery. The only exception is if
his wife had been unfaithful and had sexual
relations with another man. And whoever marries a person who has been divorced because
of marital unfaithfulness is committing adultery."
10 "If that's how it must be between a husband and his wife," His followers then spoke
up, "it's really better not to get married."
11 "Not everyone would agree with you about
that," Jesus replied; "only those who have been
given the grace to stay single.
12 "Because there are some who cannot bring
a marriage to completion because they were
born eunuchs. Others have been made
eunuchs by men. And others stay single for the
sake of promoting the Kingdom of heaven.
Allow those who are able to abstain to do so."

18:22a Luke 17:3-4.
18:24a Or *ten thousand talents of silver*. This is figured according to the weight of a Jewish talent of that day, which was 94 pounds. Troy ounces, 12 to the pound, are used in this calculation. If 16 ounces to the pound, the amount of silver owed would be 15 million ounces.
18:28a Less than twenty ounces of silver.
18:35a See 6:14; Mark 11:25-26; esp. Luke 17:3-4. Is there a debt of some kind that you also need to forgive. Consider all that God has forgiven you. What will God's judgment be in this regard concerning you?
19:4a Genesis 1:27; 5:2.
19:5a Genesis 2:24.
19:8a See Mark 10:5 note.

Jesus Welcomes the Little Children

[13] Then little children were brought to Him, so that He might place His hands on them and pray for them. But His followers scolded the people and told them to stop bothering Jesus with little children.
[14] "Let the little children come to Me!" Jesus corrected them. "Don't stop them! Because the Kingdom of heaven belongs to those who become like these little ones."[a]
[15] After He had placed His hands on the children and blessed them, He left the area.

A Rich Man's Question

[16] Once a man came to Jesus and said, "Good Teacher, what good thing must I do so that I may live forever?"
[17] "Why do you call Me 'good'?" Jesus asked. "No one is truly good except One, and that is God. But if you desire to enter into everlasting life, obey God's commands."
[18] "Which ones?" the man asked.

Jesus replied, "'Don't murder. Don't commit adultery.[a] Don't steal. Don't tell lies about anyone.
[19] 'Honor your father and mother.[a] And love others in the same way that you love yourself.'[b]"
[20] "I've obeyed all of these from the time I was a youngster," the young man said. "What else must I do?"
[21] "If you want to be perfect," Jesus replied, "go and sell what you own and give the money to the poor. By doing so you will be transferring your investments to heaven. Then come and follow Me."
[22] When the young man heard this, he walked away with a heavy heart, because he was very rich.[a]
[23] "I tell you the truth," Jesus then said to His followers, "it will be very hard for a rich person to enter the Kingdom of Heaven.
[24] "It's easier, in fact, for a camel to go through the eye of a needle than for a rich person to enter the Kingdom of God."
[25] When His followers heard that, they were utterly amazed, and questioned, "Well, who then can be saved?"[a]
[26] Looking straight at them Jesus replied, "Yes, it's impossible for people who look at money from man's sense of values to be saved, but not for the one who draws near to God and gladly receives his orders from Him. Because when even a rich person continues to live in close fellowship with God, everything is possible."[a]
[27] Peter then spoke up, "Look, we've left everything and followed You, so what will our situation be?"
[28] "I tell you the truth," Jesus replied, "when the earth and everything in it has been restored to its original perfect state, and the Son of Man is sitting on the throne of His glory, you who have followed Me will also sit on twelve thrones, judging the twelve tribes of Israel.
[29] "And everyone else who has left houses or brothers or sisters or father or mother or wife or children or lands, for My sake, will receive a hundred times more than he gave up, and will inherit everlasting life.[a]
[30] "But many who are now first will then be last, and many who are now last will be first.[a]

Parable of the Vineyard Workers

20 "Because the Kingdom of heaven is like a farmer who went out early one morning to hire men to work for him.
[2] "After he had agreed to pay them the usual amount for a day's work, he sent them into his vineyard.
[3] "About nine o'clock he went out again and found others standing around in the marketplace.
[4] "So He said to them, 'I want you men working for me as well. I'll pay you whatever is a fair.' And they went to work.
[5] "Then at twelve and again at three o'clock, he did the same.
[6] "When it was almost five o'clock he went out and found still others standing idle. 'Why have you men been wasting your time standing here all day doing nothing?' He asked them.
[7] 'No one hired us,' they replied.

'Go to work in my vineyard,' he said, 'and I'll pay you whatever is right.'
[8] "So when evening came, the owner of the vineyard said to his foreman, 'Call the workers

---

19:14a Matthew 18:1-4, and note.

19:18a See v 9.

19:19a *...by loving obedience during your childhood and youth, and by providing for them when they are sick, weary, old and feeble.* One of the greatest provisions you can give them is your sincere love and friendship, at all times. Exodus 20:12-16; Deut. 5:16-20.

19:19b Leviticus 19:18.

19:22a See Mark 10:22,25 notes.

19:25a Wealth was considered by the Jews to be a sign of blessing and approval by God. If these men, approved by God, couldn't make it to heaven, they questioned, who could?

19:26a See Luke 18:27 note.

19:27-29a Mark 10:29-30; Luke 18:28-30.

19:27-30a See Mark 10:28-31 note.

and pay them their wages. Begin with those
hired last and end with those I hired first.'
9 "When those hired about five o'clock came
before the foreman, they each received a full
day's wage.
10 "So when those hired first came before
him, they supposed they would receive more,
but they were paid the same as the others.
11 "Upon receiving it they protested to the
owner of the vineyard.
12 'These men worked only one hour,' they
bitterly complained. 'And still you've paid
them the same as those of us who worked hard
all day in the hot sun!'
13 'Listen, friend,' he answered one of them,
'I haven't cheated you. Didn't you agree to
work for me for one denarius?
14 'Now take what you have coming, and go.
It's my desire to give the last men hired the
same as you.
15 'Don't I have the right to do what I want
with my own money? Or are you envious
because I'm generous?'
16 "So," Jesus concluded, "the last will be first,
and the first last. Because many are being
called,[a] but only a few are chosen."[b]

For a Third Time Jesus Predicts His Death and Resurrection

17 Then as Jesus journeyed toward Jerusalem,
He took His twelve followers aside by themselves.
18 "Listen now," He said, "we are on our way
up to Jerusalem, where the Son of Man will be
betrayed and handed over to the chief priests
and teachers of the Law. And they will condemn Him to death.
19 "Then they will turn Him over to the
Romans, who will treat Him with utter disrespect and whip and then crucify Him. But
three days later He will rise back to life again."

A Mother's Request

20 The mother of James and John then came
to Jesus with her sons, and kneeling before
Him she said she had a request to make.
21 "What is it you want?" He asked.
"Please let one of my sons sit at Your right
hand," she said, "and the other at Your left in
Your Kingdom."
22 "You don't know what you are asking,"
Jesus replied. "Are you able to drink the bitter
mixture in the cup of the suffering and sorrow
that I am about to drink, and be baptized[a] into
the baptism into[b] which I am about to be baptized?"
"Yes, we are," James and John responded.
23 "You will indeed drink from My cup," He
replied, "and be baptized into the baptism into
which I am to be baptized, but I do not have
the authority to decide who will sit on My right
and on My left. My Father has prepared those
positions, and He will decide who will fill
them.[a]
24 When the other ten heard this request, they
were thoroughly disgusted with the two brothers.
25 So Jesus called them together, and said,
"You know how heathen rulers lord it over
their subjects, and how the very top rulers lord
it over those rulers.
26 "But that's not the way it's to be among
you. If any of you desires to become great,
you must be one who serves others.
27 "So if someone among you wants to be
your leader, make sure that he considers himself your slave.
28 "Let him be like the Son of Man, who did
not come to be served, but to serve, and to
give His very life as a ransom for many."

Two Blind Men Receive their Sight

29 As they were leaving Jericho, a huge crowd
was following Him.
30 And when two blind men sitting beside the
road heard that it was Jesus who was passing
by, they started shouting loudly, "Oh Sir, Son
of David! Have pity on us!"
31 "Stop that! Calm down!" the crowd scolded them. But instead, they shouted even loud-

---

20:16a ... *to labor in My vineyard, and all will be rewarded as I have promised* ...

20:16b ... *to shine like the stars forever and ever*. Daniel 12:3.

20:22a Baptized means *immersed*. Here, immersed into awful suffering.

20:22b ... into *the death into* ...

20:20-23a The statement of Jesus at the end of these verses should be an overwhelming inspiration and challenge to every Christian alive today. Those positions of highest honor will certainly be awarded to the two persons who are most worthy of them. No Christian is too old or too young to so wholly dedicate himself to the Lord that he might be one of those chosen to sit at the right hand or at the left hand of Christ in His Kingdom. Such promises of positions of honor, of glory, and of privilege in future service should overwhelmingly challenge every Christian to so live and serve now that he might attain to as high a position as possible in the Lord's coming Kingdom.

er, "Oh Sir, Son of David! Have pity on us!"

32 So Jesus stopped and called them to Himself, and said, "What do you want me to do for you?"

33 "Sir," they said, "we want to be able to see!"

34 Jesus was deeply moved with pity for them, so He touched their eyes. And immediately they could see, and they, too, then joyfully followed Him down the road.

The Triumphal Entry into Jerusalem

21 As they were approaching Jerusalem, and came to Bethphage near the Mount of Olives, Jesus sent two of His followers on an errand.

2 "Go into the town up ahead," He told them. "As soon as you get there you'll find a donkey tied up, and a colt with her. Untie them and bring them to Me.

3 "If anyone asks why you are untying them, tell him, 'Their true Owner[a] needs them,' and he will immediately let you take them."

4 All of this was done so that the saying of the prophet would be fulfilled, who said:

5 "Tell the people of Jerusalem, 'Look, your King is coming to you! He is humble, riding on a donkey, and on a colt, the offspring of a beast of burden.'"[a]

6 So the two went ahead and did as Jesus had told them.

7 They brought the donkey and the colt, laid their robes on them, and Jesus sat on them.[a]

8 Then most of the crowd that had gathered spread their robes on the road, while others cut branches from the trees and spread them on the road.

9 Then the crowds ahead, as well as those behind, began to shout:

"Hosanna[a] to the Son of David! 'God bless the One who comes in the name of the Lord!'[b] Hosanna in the highest heavens!"

10 When He entered Jerusalem, the whole city went wild with excitement, and everyone began asking, "Who is this?"

11 The crowds with Him replied, "This is Jesus, the prophet from Nazareth in Galilee!"

A Violent Encounter at the Temple

12 Then Jesus went into the temple area and angrily drove out those who were buying and selling there. He overturned the tables of the money changers and knocked down the benches of those selling pigeons.[a]

13 "It is written in the Scriptures that God has said, 'My House shall be called a House of Prayer,'[a]" He passionately protested, "but you have turned it into 'a place for thieves to do business'[b]!"

14 Then those who were blind and lame came to Him there in the temple area, and He healed them.

15 But when the chief priests and teachers of the Law saw the wonders he was performing, and heard the children shouting, "Hosanna to the Son of David!" they were indignant.

16 "Do you hear what these children are saying?" they angrily challenged Him.

"Yes," He replied, "haven't you ever read the Scripture:

'You have determined that You will receive praise even from the mouths of little children and infants'[a]?"

17 Then He left them and went out of the city

21:3a Literally *the Lord of them.*

21:5a Zechariah 9:9.

21:7a This indicates clearly that Jesus rode both the donkey and her colt. Some propose that Jesus rode the old donkey until He came to the place on the Mount of Olives where He wept over Jerusalem. Luke 19:41-44. Then He got off the old donkey and mounted the colt. This could symbolize God's dealing with Israel through the Old Agreement, and now entering into a New Agreement with them. Jeremiah 31:31-33; Hebrews 10:16-18. The Church does not replace Israel in God's New Agreement, but rather participates with Israel.

Many of the translations omit the *and* in the phrase *and on a colt* in v 5, but the *and* should be retained. It's in all the Greek texts, and in the Hebrew in Zechariah 9:9. The word *and* in Greek can be translated *even*, but not in this context, where both the donkey and her colt were brought to Jesus. And the Greek is definitely plural in v 7 where it says that "Jesus sat on *them.*"

21:9a Hosanna means *save now.* It later became an exclamation of praise.

21:9b Psalm 118:25-26.

21:12a The selling of animals and birds for sacrificing was legitimate, and also the exchanging of Roman for Jewish coins, but not the greedy merchandising that was evidently going on.

21:13a Isaiah 56:7.

21:13b Jeremiah 7:11. These merchants were selling birds and animals to the visiting pilgrims to sacrifice. But they were taking advantage of them and robbing them by charging exorbitant prices. The exorbitant prices charged the public by some professional and business people today comes under the same solemn indictment.

21:16a Psalm 8:2.

and went to Bethany, where He spent the
night.

A Fig Tree Miraculously Withers

18 As He was returning to the city early the
next morning, He was hungry.
19 Seeing a fig tree by the side of the road, He
went up to it. But finding nothing on it but
leaves, He said to it, "May you never bear fruit
again." And instantly that fig tree dried up!

The Lesson from the Withered Fig Tree

20 When His followers saw this happen, they
were amazed. "How could that fig tree dry up
so quickly?" they questioned.
21 "I tell you the truth," Jesus replied, "if you
have faith, and don't doubt and waver, you
will not only do what was done to that fig tree,
but more. Even if you should say to this mountain,
'Get up from here and throw yourself into
the sea,' it will happen.
22 "And that applies to everything. Whatever
you ask for in prayer, you will receive—if you
continue to believe."

Jesus' Authority Challenged

23 As Jesus was teaching the people after coming
into the temple area, the chief priests and
the elders of the people came right up to Him.
"What right do you think you have to do the
things you did here in the temple yesterday?"
they demanded. "Who gave you such authority?"
24 "I will also ask you a question," Jesus
replied. "If you answer Me, then I'll also
answer you and tell you where I got the authority
to do what I did.
25 "Who gave John the right to baptize people?
Did he get it from God, or was it just his
own idea?"

They thought about the matter, and then
said among themselves, "What shall we say?
If we say, 'From God,' He will ask us, 'Then
why didn't you believe him?'
26 "But if we say, 'It was his own idea,' this
whole mob would tear us apart, because
they're all convinced that John was a prophet."
27 So their answer to Jesus was, "We don't
know."

"And neither will I tell you where I got the
right to do what I'm doing," Jesus replied.

Faithful and Unfaithful Sons

28 "But what do you think of this? A man
with two sons went to the older son and said,
'Son, go out and work today in my vineyard.'
29 "But the son answered, 'No, I won't!' Later
he was sorry and changed his mind and went.
30 "The man then said the same thing to his
younger son. 'Sure, I'll go,' he said. But he didn't.
31 "Which of the two did what his father wanted?"

"The older one," they replied.

"And I tell you the truth," Jesus responded,
"that the despised tax collectors[a] and
whores are making more certain that they enter
the Kingdom of God than you are.
32 "Because John the Baptizer came to lead
you to live to please God. But you wouldn't
believe that God had sent him, and accept his
message. But the despised national traitors[a]
and whores did. Even after you saw the results
of John's message in changing the lives of these
sinners you didn't turn from your sinning and
live what he preached.

Murderous Sharecroppers to be Replaced

33 "Listen to another comparison: A landowner
planted a vineyard. He built a wall around
it, dug a hole for a winepress, and built a
watchtower. Then he rented it out to sharecroppers
and left the area.
34 "When it was time to harvest the grapes he
sent his servants to the sharecroppers to
receive his share of the harvest.
35 "But the sharecroppers attacked the servants.
They beat one up, killed another, and
threw stones at a third.
36 "He sent other servants—more than at
first—but the same happened to them.
37 "Finally he sent his son to them, saying,
'They will respect my son.'
38 "But when the renters saw the son coming,
they said to each other, 'Look! Here comes
the heir! Come on, let's kill him. Then we'll
get this vineyard for ourselves that he would
otherwise inherit.'
39 "So they grabbed him, dragged him out of
the vineyard and killed him.
40 "What do you suppose, therefore, the
owner of the vineyard will do to those renters
when he comes?"
41 "He will cause those wretches to suffer miserably,
and then destroy them," they replied.
"Then he will rent his vineyard to other sharecroppers
who will give him his share of the harvest
at the proper time."
42 Jesus then said, "Have you never read in
the Scriptures:

21:31 & 32a These were Jews collecting taxes from their own people for Rome.

21:42a Psalm 118:22-23. In the Passover

'The Stone that the builders threw out as worthless has become the Chief Cornerstone. This was done by the Lord, and it is marvelous to consider and look into'[a]?

43 "And it's for that reason, I tell you, the Kingdom of God will be taken from you and given to a people who will give God His rightful and proper harvest.[a]

44 "Whoever falls on this Stone will be broken, but on whoever it falls, it will grind him to powder!"[a]

45 After listening to His parables, the chief priests and Pharisees realized He was speaking about them.

46 But when they wanted to arrest Him, they were afraid to, because the great crowds there considered Him a prophet.

The Wedding Banquet

22 Then Jesus spoke to the people again, using parables. He said:

2 "The Kingdom of heaven is like what happened when a king prepared a great wedding banquet for his son.

3 "When he sent some servants out to tell the invited guests that the banquet was now ready, they refused to come.

4 "So he sent out other servants, instructing them, 'Tell my guests, "Look, dinner is ready! My choice roasts are turning on the barbecue spits, and everything is ready. Come now to the wedding banquet."'

5 "But they paid no attention. One went to his farm, another to his place of business.

6 "Others grabbed hold of his servants and beat them up, and then killed them.

7 "When the king heard about it, he flew into a rage and ordered his armies out and destroyed those murderers and burned their city.

8 "Then he said to his servants, 'The wedding banquet is ready, but those who were invited didn't deserve enjoying this pleasure.

9 'Go out now into the streets and invite everyone you find there to the wedding.'

10 "So his servants did just that. They went out on the streets and invited everyone they could find, both good and bad. So the wedding hall was filled with guests.

11 "But when the king came in to greet his guests, he saw that one man wasn't wearing a wedding robe.

12 'Friend,' he said, 'how did you get in here without wearing a wedding robe[a]?' The man was speechless.

13 "Then the king said to his servants, 'Tie him up, hand and foot, and throw him into the outer darkness, where there will be weeping and gnashing of teeth.'

14 "Because many are invited, but only a few are the chosen ones."[a]

---

seder (service) to this day this psalm is sung in the concluding part of the seder. At His first coming, Messiah was rejected by His own people. But God has made Messiah to be the Cornerstone of His Kingdom on earth.

The Jewish historian Neander said that by the end of the first century A.D. more than one million followers of the Messiah were Jewish. So not all Jews rejected Him. The first church was entirely Jewish.

21:43a This prophecy has already been fulfilled. The Kingdom of God was taken from the Jews long ago and given to the Gentiles (the non-Jewish people). It is mainly among the Gentiles that Christ has been received. But a day is coming—soon now, we trust—when great numbers among the people of Israel will also turn to Christ. Revelation 7:1-8. At this writing there has already been a great increase in converts to their Messiah among the Jewish people.

21:44a All who cast themselves on Christ, the rock of humanity's salvation, and seek mercy from Him, must do so with such abandon that they are completely broken in their rebellion and self-will. Without this death to self, there is no conversion, no born-again experience. Mark 8:34-38. Those who reject His mercy and reject His Lordship over their lives will experience the awful descending blow of judgment. They will be crushed at last by the Supreme Judge of the earth.

22:12a A white robe was provided by the host on such occasions. To spurn the robe offered was an expression of highest contempt. In this parable the robe represents the right standing with God provided by Him through Jesus Christ. Those refusing to wear this robe will be rejected by God and thrown into outer darkness.

22:14a Those chosen by God to eternal life (Romans 8:29; 1 Peter 1:2) are those whom He foreknew would be determined to meet His conditions for being born again (Matthew 11:12; John 3:1-8): by trusting in Jesus as their Savior; and obeying Him as their Lord, by turning from their sinning to living in obedience to Him, obeying both what He has told us to be busy doing, as well as what He has told us to keep from doing. Only those who are determined to enter heaven will gain entrance there. 11:12.

The Question about Paying Taxes

15 The Pharisees then left and began plotting how they could trick Jesus into saying something for which they could have Him arrested.

16 So they sent some of their men to Him along with some of Herod's followers.[a] "Teacher," they said, "we know that You always tell the truth, and you also teach the truth about what God wants us to know and do. We know you're not trying to gain the favor of anyone, and that you're not swayed by the importance of anyone.

17 "So would you give us your opinion on a matter? Is it right, according to the Laws that God has given us, for us Jews to pay taxes to the Roman Emperor, or should we refuse to pay them?"[a]

18 But Jesus knew what their evil plan was, so He said, "You hypocrites! Why are you trying to trap Me?

19 "Show Me the coin you use to pay the tax." So they brought Him a denarius.

20 "Whose picture and name are these on here?" He asked.

21 "The Emperor's," they replied.

"Then give the Emperor what belongs to him," He said, "and give to God what belongs to God."

22 Upon hearing that, they were stunned. And they left Him and went their way.

On Marriage after the Resurrection

23 That same day the Sadducees, who say that no one who dies will come back to life again, came to Him with a question.

24 "Teacher," they said, "Moses said that if a man dies without having any children, his brother must marry the widow, and raise up a child for his brother.[a]

25 "We had a case here involving seven brothers. The first one married, but he died before having any children, so he left his wife to his brother.

26 "The same thing happened to the second brother, and the third, and on down to the seventh.

27 "Finally, the woman died.

28 "So which of the seven brothers will be married to her after the resurrection? Because she was the wife of all of them."

29 "You are mistaken," Jesus replied, "because you don't know what the Scriptures teach about the resurrection.[a] And you don't realize how powerful God is.[b]

30 "After the resurrection no one will marry or be given in marriage. In heaven everyone will be like God's angels.

31 "As for the resurrection of the dead, haven't you read what God told you about that, when He said,

32 'I am the God worshiped by Abraham, Isaac, and Jacob'[a]? He is not the God of dead people, but of those who are very much alive!"

33 When the crowd heard this, they were amazed at the knowledge and wisdom of His teaching.

The Greatest Command of God

34 When the Pharisees heard that Jesus had silenced the Sadducees, they got together for another strategy session.

35 Then one of them, who was an expert in the Law of Moses, asked Him another question to try to trap Him.

36 "Teacher," he said, "which is the most important command in the Law?"

37 Jesus replied,

"'You shall love the Lord your God with all your heart, with all your soul, and with all your mind.'[a]

38 "This is the most important and the greatest of all of God's commands.

39 "The second most important is like it:

'You shall love others in the same way that you love yourself.'[a]

40 "The entire Law of Moses and all the writings of the prophets are founded upon the principles contained in these two commands."

A Question about the Messiah

41 While the Pharisees were gathered together there, Jesus, in turn asked them a question.

42 "What is your opinion about the Messiah?" He asked them. "What family will He come from?"

They are the ones who are indeed born again. They realize full well that mere selective obedience will not gain them entrance into heaven. See Appendix 211.

22:16a See Mark 3:6 note.

22:17a As the Passover lamb was examined for four days before Passover, so Jesus was examined by the religious leaders of the nation through intense questioning.

22:24a ... *to inherit his property.*

22:29a See v 32 and Job 19:25-27; Isaiah 26:19; Daniel 12:2.

22:29b There is absolutely nothing too hard for God. Whatever He has promised, He will do. Therefore the dead definitely will be raised. Genesis 18:14a.

22:32a Exodus 3:6,15.

22:37a Deuteronomy 6:5.

22:39a Leviticus 19:18.

"He'll be a descendant of King David," they
replied.
43 "How is it then," He questioned, "that,
inspired by the Holy Spirit, David calls Him
'Lord'? Because David said:
44 'God said to My Lord,[a] "Sit at My right
hand until I make Your enemies into a footstool for Your feet."'[b]
45 "Now if David called Him 'Lord,' how can
He be his descendant?"[a]
46 No one had even one word to say in reply.
From then on no one dared to put any more
questions to Him.

The Jewish Leaders Condemned

23 Then Jesus said to the crowds and to
His followers:
2 "The Pharisees and the teachers of the Law
are experts in explaining what the Law of
Moses teaches.
3 "So whatever they explain to you about the
Law, be sure that you pay close attention and
follow their instructions and do as they direct.
But don't do what they do, because they don't
practice what they teach.
4 "They put heavy loads of religious require-
ments on people's backs, that are hard to carry,
but they won't use even one of their own fin-
gers to lift and ease the burden.
5 "Everything they do is for the purpose of
drawing attention to themselves. Notice how
they have enlarged the little boxes containing
Scriptures to be worn on the forehead and
arm. Also notice how long they have made the
fringes on their robes.
6 "They love a place at the head table at ban-
quets, and the prominent seats in the synagogue.
7 "And, oh, how they love to be greeted with
respect in the marketplaces and have people
call them 'Master'[a].
8 "But none of you should be called 'Master',
because you have only one Master, which is
the Messiah, and you are all brothers and sisters.
9 "And don't call anyone on earth 'Father',
because you have only one Father, who is in
heaven.
10 "Nor are you to be called 'Leader', because
you have only one Leader, who is the Messiah.
11 "The greatest among you will be the one
who serves you.
12 "So whoever promotes himself will be
pulled down. But whoever humbly helps others will be honored.

The Leaders' Hypocrisy Condemned

13 "Woe to you Pharisees and teachers of the
Law! You hypocrites! Because you shut the
door to the Kingdom of Heaven in people's
faces. Not only are you not entering it yourselves, but when others try to enter, you stop
them.
14 "Woe to you Pharisees and teachers of the
Law! You hypocrites! You cheat widows out
of their homes and other properties, and then
pretend to be so holy by your long prayers.
Therefore your sentence on Judgment Day will
be even greater than what's given other sinners.
15 "Woe to you Pharisees and teachers of the
Law! You hypocrites! You travel to the ends of
the earth to win one convert, and after you win
him, you make him twice as fit for hell as you
are yourselves.
16 "Woe to you, you blind guides, who say,
'You don't need to fulfill your promise when
you make a promise by swearing by the temple; but whoever swears to God concerning a
future gift of gold he vows to bring to the temple is obligated to fulfill his promise.'[a]
17 "You blind fools! Which is greater, the
gold, or the temple that makes the gold sacred?
18 "You also say, 'You don't need to fulfill
your promise when you make a promise by
swearing by the altar; but whoever swears by
the gift he vows to sacrifice to God there, is
obligated to perform his oath.'[a]
19 "You blind fools! Which is greater, the gift,
or the altar that makes the gift sacred?
20 "So the one who swears by the altar also
swears by everything on it.
21 "And the one who swears by the temple
also swears by God, who lives there.
22 "And the one who swears by heaven,
swears by the throne of God and by the One
who sits on that throne.
23 "Woe to you Pharisees and teachers of the
Law! You hypocrites! You give God a tenth of
even the spices from your garden, such as

22:44a This was God the Father speaking to God the Son.

22:44b Psalm 110:1.

22:45a Christ is actually the Son of God, therefore David's Lord. But He took on human form, and received His human body through the ancestry of David. For that reason He is called the Son of David, or, a descendant of David.

23:7a The word *Rabbi* was an honorary title which meant *Lord, Master, Great Teacher*, or *My Lord*, for outstanding teachers of the Law.

23:16a See 15:5.

23:18a See Mark 7:11 note.

mint, dill, and cumin. But you have neglected to obey the more important matters of the Law, such as justice, mercy, and honesty. You should do the good you are doing, but not to the neglect of these more important matters!

24 "You blind guides! You strain out a tiny fly from your soup, but swallow a camel![a]

25 "Woe to you Pharisees and teachers of the Law! You hypocrites! You wash the outside of your cups and dishes so diligently, but inside yourselves you are rotten with the filth of cheating others and thinking only of yourselves.

26 "You blind Pharisees! First clean the inside of the cup and dish, then the outside will also be clean.[a]

27 "Woe to you Pharisees and teachers of the Law! You hypocrites! You are like white marble tombs, beautiful on the outside, but inside, full of dead men's bones and other filth.

28 "In the same way, your outward appearance causes people to believe you are so pure and honest, but inside you are full of pretense and rebellion against what God wants you to be and do.

29 "Woe to you Pharisees and teachers of the Law! You hypocrites! You build monuments for the prophets and decorate the tombs of those who lived good lives,

30 and then you say, 'If we had lived when our ancestors did, we wouldn't have had any part in killing the prophets.'

31 "But you witness against yourselves, because you admit that you are the children of those who murdered the prophets.

Their Awful Punishment Predicted

32 "Go ahead! Fill up to the top the measuring cup which already holds the sins of your fathers![a]

33 "You snakes! You children of vipers! How can you expect to escape being condemned to hell?

34 "For that reason I will indeed send you prophets[a] and wise men and teachers.[b] But you will kill some, and nail others to a cross. Others you will whip in your synagogues, and then chase and persecute from one city to the next.

35 "For that reason the punishment due for the murder of godly men throughout the whole world will fall on you—from the murder of righteous Abel, to the murder of Zechariah, son of Berechiah, whom you murdered between the temple and the altar.

36 "I tell you the truth, the total of all the judgments for all these atrocities over the centuries will fall upon you people who are alive today![a]

Jesus' Love for Jerusalem

37 "O Jerusalem! Jerusalem! You who have killed the prophets and stoned to death the messengers sent to you! How often I have wanted to gather your people together, as a hen gathers her chicks under her wings, but you were not willing.

38 "Look! Your temple is about to be utterly abandoned by God.[a]

39 "I tell you, there is no way that you will see Me again until the day when you will say, 'How wonderful and blessed by God is the One who comes in the name of the Lord.'[a]"

Destruction of Jerusalem Predicted

24 As Jesus was leaving the temple area, some of His followers[a] came up to Him to point out some of the interesting things about the temple buildings.

2 "Yes, take a good look at these beautiful buildings," Jesus responded, "because I tell you the truth, when Jerusalem is destroyed,[a] not one stone will be left upon another. They will all be torn down."

The Signs of the End of the Age

3 Later, as He was sitting on the Mount of Olives, some of His followers[a] went to speak

---

23:24a They placed such importance upon little things, but ignored the truly important things.

23:26a First clean the inside (your heart), then the outside (the things you say and do), will also be clean.

23:32a This was a prediction of what they were about to do to Jesus. He was saying, in effect, "By slaying Me, fill up what is lacking in the sins of your fathers until the measuring cup is full—until as much has been committed as God can possibly bear. But then you must take the consequences." And they have been taking the consequences ever since A.D. 70.

23:34a Or *preachers.*

23:34b ... *in an endeavor to awaken you to the truth.*

23:36a The horrendous slaughter and destruction of Jerusalem took place less than 40 years later, in A.D. 70. The Romans killed well over a million Jews during the siege and burned the city, and drove almost 100,000 Jews into captivity.

23:38a See 24:1-2.

23:39a Psalm 118:26.

24:1a Mark 13:1 states that it was one follower who did the speaking.

24:2a See 23:36 note.

24:3a Mark 13:3 reveals that only Peter,

to Him privately. "Tell us," they said. "When will all these things happen? And what will happen to alert us that You are soon coming again, and that the end of the age is near?"[b]

4 "One of the main things," Jesus replied, "is to be on your guard so that no one fools you.

5 "Because many will come claiming to be Me, saying, 'I am the Christ,' and many will be fooled.[a]

6 "And you will hear of wars, and rumors of more wars, but don't be alarmed. All of these events must take place, but they do not mean that the end has come.

7 "*Because when the end is actually approaching,*[a] nations will rise up and war against other nations, and kingdoms against other kingdoms. And there will be famines, disease epidemics, and earthquakes in various places.

8 "But even these are only the beginning of the birth pangs.[a]

9 "Then they will hand you over to be fright-

James, John, and Andrew were sufficiently interested to question Jesus about His startling statements in front of the temple. Luke 21:5-36

24:3b Christ was approached twice that day by His followers concerning some amazing statements He had just made. According to Luke 21:7, it appears that Christ gave the prophecy recorded there, to all who were standing near Him outside the temple. Now, when Christ had left the temple and was on His way to Bethany, having reached the top of *the Mount of Olives,* He sat down. Mark 13:3 informs us that it was at this location that four of Jesus' followers—Peter, James, John, and Andrew—*asked Him privately* to explain more fully what He had said in front of the temple. They wanted the inside, full story.

At the temple, the people listening had asked Jesus what would alert them of the impending destruction of the temple, about which He has just told them. Luke 21:6-7. He answered their question (Luke 21:12-24), also adding some details about His second coming. Luke 21:8-11, 25-32. Afterward, *on the mount of Olives,* these four followers approached Him to ask for more details concerning His brief mention of His *second coming. "Tell us," they said, "when will all these things happen,* these things you just referred to in front of the temple, *and what will happen to alert us that you are soon coming again, and that the end of the age is near?"* In front of the temple, Jesus had been asked for a sign that would alert them that the great temple building was about to be destroyed. Luke 21:7. Now, He is asked for a sign that would alert them concerning the end of the age and of His returning in *power and great glory.* Luke 21:25-28.

24:4-5a The Lord again warns His followers, as He had in front of the temple (Luke 21:8), of possible deception. As He stood before the temple (Luke 21:20-24), Jesus dealt with the subject of the destruction of Jerusalem, which took place in A.D. 70. Several historians, *including Josephus,* wrote that there arose a number of imposters claiming to be the Messiah between the time of Christ's resurrection and the destruction of Jerusalem. Some of the people were deceived by these men.

Even though *false Christs* arose in that era, a double fulfillment of this prophecy, as is true of many other prophecies, is to be expected. "A.C. Gaebelein says that the false Christs of other days and of today (1924) are but faint shadows of what will take place in the end time soon to come."—*Biederwolf, in The Millennium Bible.*

And today, as the end is fast approaching, there are many men claiming to be Jesus Christ. No doubt, their numbers will continue to increase.

24:7a Implied.

24:6-8a Jesus now tells His followers how they would be able to discern when the world was entering into *the beginning of the birth pangs.* He tells how they would be able to discern the beginning of the birth pangs that would bring about the rebirth of Israel and ultimately result in the establishment of the Kingdom of God on earth. The approach of the end of the age would be heralded by several phenomena on the earth occurring simultaneously. Those phenomena, as listed by Jesus are: 1. *Nation rising up against nation* 2. *Kingdom rising against Kingdom* 3. *Famines* 4. *Disease epidemics* 5. *Earthquakes in various places.* In Mark 13 the word *troubles* is used by our Lord instead of disease epidemics. It could be that the Lord used both words.

* * *

Wars between *nations,* or even between *kingdoms,* is and has been a common occurrence. History has recorded *famines* at various times. There have been times of great *disease epidemics.* There have been *earthquakes* in the past, but increasingly so in the present day. Jesus tells His disciples, however, to be awaiting a specific time during which all of these phenomena would be in evidence at the same time. The first such time in world history occurred during the years of World War I (1914-1918) and

fully mistreated, tortured, and put to death. You will be hated by people in all nations because of your solid allegiance to My name.[a]
10 "At that time many will give up and turn away from their faith in Me, and betray and hate one another.
11 "Many false prophets will also appear on the scene and will fool many.[a]

---

immediately following.

World War I broke out when the heir apparent to the Austrian throne was assassinated by a Serbian zealot. Hostilities between the two countries over this incident resulted in Austria declaring war on Serbia one month later. This was *nation against nation*. Shortly after this the *nations and kingdoms* of the world chose sides and entered the war. Before the war had ended, four years later, 43 of the principal nations of the world had entered the conflict. It was a vastly greater conflict than had ever before been waged on earth. In other conflicts hundred of thousands had been involved, but in World War I there were tens of millions in uniform. Never before had so many *nations risen up against nations* and *kingdoms against kingdoms*—all involved in the same war.

* * *

Widespread *famine* in many areas followed World War I. Many homes today still remember the loss of a loved one in the *disease epidemic* of that same time—the terrible flu epidemic raged out of control. About 20 million people, including more than 500,000 Americans, died in this epidemic in 1918-1919. *Earthquakes* not only took their toll but have occurred with increasing frequency throughout the world from that time until now.

World War I, then, was evidently *the beginning of the birth pangs* that would give rebirth to Israel and eventually give birth to God's Kingdom on earth, as well. It was during World War I that the wheels were set in motion to bring about the rebirth of Israel as a nation. Israel will one day be born spiritually as a nation, at the return of Christ (Isaiah 66:7-9), but in 1948 she came to full birth as a nation in modern times. And at this writing she again controls her own land.

24:9a This means, *because you believe and are living all that My name* (the Lord Jesus Christ) *implies. You are obeying Me as your Lord, you are trusting Me as your Savior* (the meaning of the name Jesus), and *you believe Me to be the Christ* (the One chosen, anointed and blessed by God—the coming King of all the earth). Acts 16:31. It costs something to be a Christian. In the days ahead it may very likely cost you tribulation and death. But your resurrection to eternal life will be worth being hated and killed a million times over for your Lord and Savior. It has been rightly said, *When you get to heaven, the Lord won't look you over for degrees but for scars.*

* * *

This verse is another example of the two's of the Bible. In His discourse in front of the temple, as recorded in Luke 21:12-19, the Lord prophesied imminent persecution for His followers. Here He goes beyond their immediate future, to tell of their final persecution in the end time. This last attack on Christians would correspond to *the beginning of the birth pangs*. The word *then* means, *at that time*, at the time of *the beginning of birth pangs*. Christians have been persecuted since the time of Christ, and especially during the first 300 years following His crucifixion and resurrection. Multiplied thousands upon thousands were martyred during those years. But following the beginning of World War I, there have already been more martyrs of the Christian faith than the total of all previous Christian martyrs. These martyrdoms have occurred mainly in Russia, China, eastern Europe, South America, and Asia. But the end is not yet. The prophecy states that *you will be hated by all nations, because of your solid allegiance to My name*. The time is coming when every true Christian throughout the world will be a marked person. In addition to being hated, followers of Jesus are likely to be martyred by the hundreds of thousands and by the millions in days to come. See also Mark 13:9-13; Daniel 7:20-22,25; 8:24; 11:32-35; 12:7b; Revelation 13:7.

A reading of the above Scriptures will reveal that Antichrist will wage war against all true followers of the Lord when he comes on the scene. And when he has finally succeeded in conquering them, then the Lord will return and send him to his place. Revelation 19:11-21.

24:11a There have been *false prophets* from the beginning of the early Church, and throughout the centuries. Today, however, false cults and *false prophets* are literally flooding the land and the world in a greater than ever tide. No doubt their number will continue to increase. Included among the false prophets are those preachers who are preaching an easy way to heaven—which will not get you there! Sadly, our Lord's prophecy that they *will deceive many* is also coming true.

12 "And because people will be sinning everywhere and in every way, multiplied times
worse than ever before, even many of my followers will grow cold in their love for Me.[a]
13 "But those who remain faithful to Me to the
end of life will be saved.[a]
14 "*In spite of the great falling away*,[a] the
Great News about the Kingdom of Christ[b] will
be preached throughout the whole world, and
solemnly declared in every nation. Then the
end will come.

The Sign to Flee Judea

15 "So when you see the abominable thing
that represents the one who has caused so
much devastation, standing now in the temple
area, just as the prophet Daniel said would happen (let whoever reads Daniel give diligence to
understand what he is saying),[a]
16 "then those in Judea must flee to the hills!

24:12a See God's warning to such, in Revelation 3:16.

24:13a 11:22.

24:14a Implied.

24:14b The Great News about salvation through Jesus Christ, and about His Kingdom, was preached to all the then-known-world by the time of the destruction of Jerusalem in A.D. 70. Once again, however, as the present age is ending, this prophecy of Jesus is being fulfilled—this time on a much larger scale. The Great News is again going forth *throughout the whole world* with emphasis on *the Kingdom message*— that Christ must be made Lord and King in one's life, and the Great News about the coming new and wonderful Kingdom of our Lord on earth.

After *the Great News about the Kingdom of Christ* has been proclaimed world-wide, *then the end will come*. That day is fast approaching, as the Great News is now being broadcast world-wide by every possible means, including radio, television, and the printed page.

24:15a The words *the abominable thing that represents the one who has caused so much devastation* come from Daniel 9:27; 11:31; and 12:11. From these verses in Daniel and from Revelation 11:1-2 we have the prophecy that the Antichrist will make a 7-year pact *with many*. In the middle of the 7-year period, he will break this treaty, (Daniel 9:27), and cause his *abominable image* to *stand in the temple area* in Jerusalem.

The words *abominable thing* are translated from the Greek word *bdelugma*, which means *something detestable, disgusting, hateful, shameful, something that stinks*. From our study of this word in Daniel 9:27, we find that it evidently refers to an idol. And we do read of an idol in reference to Antichrist in Revelation 13:14-15. Reference is made to this idol image more than once. See Revelation 14:9-11; 15:2; 16:2; 19:20; 20:4; Daniel 11:31; 12:11; Mark 13:14.

The word *devastation* is translated from the Greek word *eraymoseos*, which means *to lay waste, to bring to or make desolate*. The Jews will have built their temple in Jerusalem by this time, and the practice of sacrificing animals on the altar will have commenced again. From our study of Daniel 8:11-14 we discover that evidently what this *abominable thing* and *devastation* refers to is that when Antichrist turns against the Jews in Jerusalem (Isaiah 33:7-9), in the middle of his 7-year treaty, he will blast the altar of sacrifice out of the way and cause his image to *stand* there in its place. Revelation 13:14-15.

Be sure to read *Daniel 8:11-14* in connection with this.

* * *

Jesus ends His statement concerning the abominable thing with the following admonition: *Let whoever reads Daniel, give diligence to understand what he is saying*. The meaning of the words *abominable thing* and *devastation* have been obscure and not really understood throughout the centuries. But the time is now near at hand for the fulfillment of this *abominable thing* and *devastation*, and the Lord is making known to his people the true meaning of what will actually occur, so that believing Jews in Israel may know what to expect, and may prepare to heed our Lord's strong warning to *flee to the hills* when the *devastation* of the altar takes place and the *abominable thing* is erected in its place.

Concerning the *understanding* of these things in the last days, our Lord told Daniel (Daniel 12:10b), "And none of the wicked will understand; but the wise will understand." "The wise" refers to the true followers of Christ.

Be sure to read Zechariah 14:1-7 in regard to this. Also, don't fail to read Appendix 244, entitled, The Revealed Timetable For The End!

* * *

In 168 B.C. Antiochus Epiphanes sent General Apollonius with 22,000 soldiers to Jerusalem (pretending to come peacefully), and attacked and plundered the city. They then desecrated the altar of burnt offerings by building an altar dedicated to Zeus upon it, and killing and offering pigs upon their altar. A statue of Zeus was also erected in the temple area. But Jesus said the primary

17 "If you are out on your roof deck when you hear the news, don't go down into the house for anything at all.[a]
18 "The person in the field must not go back into the house or anywhere else to even get his clothes.[a]
19 "This will be a frightful and difficult time for those who are expectant mothers, and for those with nursing babies.[a]
20 "Pray that you won't need to escape in winter or on the Sabbath.[a]
21 "Because there will then be frightful persecution, calamity, and suffering—far greater than any other since the beginning of time until now. There will never again be anything like it.
22 "If God didn't cut that time short, there wouldn't be any life left on earth. But for the sake of God's chosen ones, He will cut that time short.[a]
23 "If anyone then tells you, 'Look! The Messiah is over here!' or 'Over there!' don't believe it.
24 "Because false messiahs and false prophets will rise up and do such amazing wonders and miracles that they will be convincing enough to deceive even God's chosen ones, if that were possible.
25 "Pay attention, and realize that I have warned you before all of this takes place.

---

fulfillment of Daniel's prophecy is yet future.

24:17a Only those who flee immediately will escape.

24:16-18a Jews living in Judea at this time are hereby warned by our Lord that when this happening is announced by radio, or seen on television (the altar removed and the image of the Antichrist erected) they are to flee out of the country without stopping for anything. It would be wise for believing families in Israel to discuss flight plans ahead of time so that when this terrible event occurs, everyone will be prepared. Anyone *going back to the house* to assist others or to save any material thing will no doubt lose his life. Our Lord's warning here indicates that it is only those who flee immediately and directly who will escape. Any person within a house is *not to go to another part of the same house* to take a single thing with him. *Those in the fields* are to head for the mountains *without returning home*. The destruction coming upon Israel at that time will be sudden and terrible. Only a small portion of the Jews will escape. Only those few who are willing to drop everything and flee according to the Lord's instructions will be saved.

* * *

In our study of Zechariah 14:1-7, we find that the Lord will cause the Mount of Olives, east of Jerusalem, to divide in the middle and provide a valley of escape for those who are willing to drop everything and flee through it. They will flee through the valley into the country of Jordan.

From the time of the *devastation* in Jerusalem until Jesus returns in power and glory to rule over this world as King of kings and Lord of lords approximately three-and-one-half years will pass. But these will be three-and-one-half years of the most terrifying tribulation the world has every known. See vss 21-22.

24:19a This flight from Judea and Jerusalem will be particularly difficult for women with children and for any woman who is about to give birth to a child. Even in such cases, however, faithful and immediate heed to the Lord's warning to flee the country will no doubt ensure escape.

24:20a Let the people of Israel take notice! The Lord encourages you to *pray* that this hour of flight will not come during the winter when the weather would make the escape most difficult, and to also *pray* that it not be on the *Sabbath day* when the orthodox Jew is allowed to travel less than a mile.

For other Scriptures concerning Israel's flight into the wilderness in Jordan see Isaiah 26:20-21; 33:2-3; 41:10-20; 44:1-7; Jeremiah 30:4-9; Ezekiel 20:35-38; Hosea 2:14-15; Micah 5:3 (1-15); Zechariah 10:11a; 12:10a; 13:8-9; 14:3-7; Mark 13:14-23; Luke 17:26-37; Revelation 12:1-6, 13-17.

24:21-22a The tribulation of the last days of this dispensation will be so devastating, with so much loss of life, that unless *that time were cut short, there would be no life left on earth*. In God's future plans He has already determined that this time will be a short time. Events will not be allowed to run their natural course, or everyone on earth would be killed. Though it is unlikely that the period of three-and-a-half years will be shortened, God will evidently curtail the frightful devastation and slaughter on the earth in some way so that mankind is not completely blotted from the face of the earth. God will show this mercy *for the sake of His elect*. The elect are all the chosen of God, whether Jew or Gentile. They are those persons who truly love Him, and obey and serve Him.

24:23-27a Christ showed His deep concern about false Christs, as He warned about them in front of the temple (Luke 21:8), at

26 "So if anyone tells you, 'Look! He's out in the desert!' don't go out there. Or if they say, 'He's in a room back there!' don't believe it.

27 "Because when the Son of Man comes, He will be as visible for everyone to clearly see as a bolt of lightning is when it flashes in the east and then brilliantly travels all the way across the sky to the west.[a]

28 "Because wherever there's a body about to die, there you will find the vultures gathered together.[a]

The Second Coming of Messiah

29 "Immediately after the tribulation of those days, the sun will be darkened, and the moon won't give its light.[a] The stars will fall from the heavens,[b] and the natural forces controlling the planets will be shaken.[c]

30 "Then the sign that will herald the coming of the Son of Man will appear in the sky! When that happens, all the people on earth will mourn.[a] Because then they will see the Son of Man whom they had spurned, coming on the clouds in the sky, with a most majestic display of power and great glory.

31 "And with a powerful trumpet blast I will send out My angels to gather My chosen ones together from the four corners of the earth, from the extremity of one horizon to the extremity of the other.[a]

---

the beginning of this discourse (vss 4-5), and now again. As we previously stated, false Christs appeared a few years after Christ's resurrection (though not many) and now again, a second time, false Christs (many of them), will appear. They will evidently be inspired by Satan, and this time given power by him, because they will perform *amazing signs and wonders*. These signs and wonders will be so convincing that even the elect will almost be fooled.

Jesus definitely states, however, that His second coming will be neither secret nor humble. Rather, the glory and brightness of His person and power (v 27) will be seen from one end of the heavens to the other. Those who are alive on earth during the coming days of sorrow need to be warned again and again to believe no one who claims to be Christ, no matter how convincing his arguments or the display of signs and wonders. Christ will not appear in resurrected form until after the time of darkness, earthquake, and fire (evidently 45 days, Daniel 12:11-12) which is to follow the Battle of Armageddon.

24:28a This verse has nothing to do with the Battle of Armageddon, as many believe. These are human vultures. And when these human vultures see Israel in distress and tribulation, viewing as well this world age in its death throes, they will go to any lengths in their attempt to further their own self interests, even to pretending to be Christ, the Messiah.

24:29a Refer to Revelation 6:12-17 for a vivid description of what will take place immediately after the tribulation and the Battle of Armageddon. Revelation 6 gives an overview of end-time happening, and vss 12-17 reveal what will take place at this momentous time in history. It is very possible that this *darkness* and the other judgments here will affect the earth and the heavens for a period of some 45 days following Armageddon, before Christ appears in the heavens. Daniel 12:11 gives us 1,290 days for the time of the tribulation. Then in the very next verse, verse 12, he states, "Blessed is he who waits, and comes to the 1335th day!" That is 45 days later. So this judgment of *darkness*, etc., may continue for a longer period than most Bible students have previously believed.

24:29b This evidently refers to showers of meteorites (large and small) crashing into the earth in a horrendous judgment.

24:29c ... *and will no longer keep those bodies in their courses*. See Isaiah 13:9-14.

24:30a *Then* at the end of this terrible time of darkness *the sign that will herald the coming of the Son of man will appear in the sky*. What a great and glorious day that will be when Christ comes to earth in His *majestic display of power and great glory* to receive His Kingdom! See Isaiah 40:5, 9-11; Zechariah 2:10-13; Matthew 26:64; Mark 13:24-26; Luke 21:27; Acts 1:9-11; Revelation 1:7-8. But what a terrible day of consternation and woe that day will be for the ungodly! Revelation 6:15-17. *All the people on earth will mourn*, because only those who have refused Christ as Savior and refused Him the lordship of their lives will be left on earth. All others by this moment will have been raptured to be with Christ.

24:31a The Apostle Paul refers to this time in 1 Corinthians 15:51-52 when he refers to the Rapture of the Church taking place *at the sounding of the last trumpet*. And this is the last trumpet prophesied to sound during the age of grace. Paul also refers to this time in 1 Thessalonians 4:15-18.

This *last trumpet* cannot be the last of the seven trumpets in the Revelation because all seven of those trumpets are trumpets bringing forth frightful judgment upon the earth.

32 "Now learn a lesson from the fig tree.
When its branches become tender and grow
leaves, you know that summer is near.[a]
33 "In the same way, when you see all these
things beginning to happen, realize that the end
is near, right at the door.[a]
34 "I tell you the truth, this generation will not
pass away before all of these things have taken
place.[a]
35 "The heavens and the earth will pass away,
but there's no possibility whatever that what I
say will come to nothing.[a]

No One Knows the Day and Hour

36 "But as for the day and the hour when each
of these events will take place, no one knows,
not even the angels in heaven. Only My
Father knows.[a]
37 "But when the Son of Man comes, things
will be just like they were in the time of Noah.
38 "During the days just before the flood, people were eating and drinking as usual. They
were getting married, and giving their daughters in marriage. Life was going on as usual
even on the very day that Noah and his family
entered the big ship he had built.
39 "They didn't know that the prophesied
flood would come that day until it came and
swept them all away. And that's exactly how it
will be when the Son of Man comes.[a]
40 "Two men at that time will be working in
the field. One will be taken away and the
other will be left behind.
41 "Two women will be together grinding
grain. One will be taken away and the other

The *last trumpet* will be an eighth trumpet that will be sounded after Armageddon, and will be a trumpet announcing great victory and extreme joy. It will herald the beginning of the reign of the Son of God upon earth as King of Kings and Lord of Lords! Being that both Christ and the Apostle Paul state that it is at this time that the Rapture will take place, why would anyone expect it to happen before? See Appendix 201 for extensive note.

24:32-34a Many claim that the *fig tree* here is symbolic of the Jewish nation. But such an interpretation fails in light of the fact that Luke 21:29 adds, *and all the other trees*. Jesus' statement was simply a matter of everyday understanding. When one sees the trees of the forest and field putting forth leaves, he knows that summer is close at hand. Likewise, when people see these prophecies of Jesus beginning to take place, they can know that the time of His harvest is near. He says, in fact, that *When you see all these things beginning to happen, realize that the end is near, right at the door*.

It will be so imminent that *this generation* (we believe He is speaking of the generation living at the time when these things begin to come to pass) *will positively not pass away before all of these things have taken place*. It is the older generation, living today, that was born when the *birth pangs* of the end of the age began (see vss 7-8). We believe it is this generation that witnessed the beginning of the end. According to Jesus' clear indication, the older generation of today will not die out until all things are fulfilled. If such is the case, the end must be very near. See Mark 13:30 note.

Some claim that the words *this generation* in v 34 refer to the generation living when Christ spoke these words. But that generation did not see *all of these things take place*. They certainly did not see the events that will follow the Great Tribulation. The only possible conclusion is that *this generation* refers to the generation living when these end time happenings begin to happen. See vss 6-8 note. These are the ones who will see the final events that will lead up to the return of Christ. It's today's older generation! So the end is rapidly approaching.

24:35a These things are so certain to come to pass that our Lord declares that even though it is true that *the heavens and the earth will pass away*, these words of His in this prophecy, and throughout the Bible, will positively not pass away. His words will be fulfilled to the very letter.

24:36a Our Lord does not tell us that we will not know the approximate time of His coming, because He has given us all kinds of signs and indications to look for which will indicate that the time is drawing near. But He does state that nobody but the Father *knows the day* or *the hour* when He will return. Even Christ did not know. Mark 13:32.

24:37-39a In the days of Noah the earth was destroyed by the great flood—God's judgment on the shocking wickedness of people upon the earth. Genesis 6-8. It may be, on one hand, that the Lord is comparing wickedness in Noah's day to wickedness in the days of His coming. On the other hand, He may simply be saying that life will go on as usual, even as it did just prior to the great flood. People will be *eating and drinking, getting married and giving their daughters in marriage, even on the very day* that judgment

left behind.[a]
42 "So you must always be ready, because you don't know what day or hour your Lord will come.
43 "Look at it this way: If the man of the house had known at what hour of the night the thief was coming, he would have been ready for him, to make sure his house wasn't broken into.
44 "For that very reason, you must always be ready, because the Son of Man is coming at a time when you will least expect Him.[a]

Faithful and Unfaithful Servants

45 "Who then is a faithful and wise servant? He is the one whom his master has put in charge of his household, to give them food at the proper time.
46 "He will be a very happy servant indeed if he is found doing what he was assigned to do when his master returns.
47 "I tell you the truth, his master will put him in charge of everything he owns.[a]
48 "But suppose that servant is evil, and says to himself, 'My master won't be here for a while yet.'
49 So he begins to bully and beat his fellow servants, and to eat and drink with his drunkard friends.
50 "The master of that servant will come back

---

from God strikes.

24:40-41a The *two men in the field* and the *two women grinding at the mill* with the *one taken and the other left* would appear to speak of judgment. Many have believed that these verses speak of the Rapture of the Church before the Great Tribulation—the true Christian being *taken* from the earth and the unbeliever *left*. It would seem, however, that this is a continuation of the judgment scene of the previous verses.

The Lord promised in Genesis 8:20-22; 9:8-17 that He would never again destroy the earth with a flood. The next judgment will be by fire 2 Peter 3:5-12. In vss 37 39 Christ referred to the previous judgment by water, and compared that event with the future judgment of this world (v 39b) by fire, earthquake, etc., both preceding and following Armageddon. Nahum 1:5; Malachi 4:1-3; 2 Peter 3:5-14; Revelation 6:12-17. Many people will be destroyed in these final judgments, while others in the same place will be spared, in order that the earth might be replenished during the Millennium. Zechariah 14:16-21; Isaiah 2:2-4. So some will *be taken* in death and some will be *left*.

* * *

During these days of awful judgment upon the earth, following the Battle of Armageddon, God will be cleansing the earth by fire, and remaking it by earthquakes, great hailstones, crashing meteorites, etc. The resultant renovated earth will contain no more islands, and the mountains will be leveled as rolling hills. Revelation 16:20. It is evident that even this final judgment will come as a surprise to most people still living on the earth. The Lord will have blinded their eyes because of their determination to continue in their sin. They will not recognize the time in which they live as being the time just previous to *the end of the world* as we know it today.

Just what criteria the Lord will use at this time to choose between those who will be *taken* and those who will be *left* is not revealed. Even among unbelievers there are degrees of wickedness and rebellion. The righteous Lord in His infinite wisdom will be quite able to choose those to be *taken* in death at this time and those to be *left* to live during the Millennium. It is impossible to determine for sure the exact meaning of those *taken* and those *left*. It certainly appears that judgment is the theme.

24:42-44a These verses also speak of judgment, especially v 43. It is no doubt because of just such a warning from Jesus that Peter was moved to write, "Be most diligent to make your calling and election to salvation and eternal life with God a sure thing." 2 Peter 1:10. We must be ready to meet Him now—today! The ungodly person who trusts that he has time to continue in his sinning, before repenting, will undoubtedly find the judgment of death upon him before he expects it.

The warning is issued, as well, to all who profess to know Christ as Lord and Savior. So much is at stake in so many lives. We have no promise of a sure tomorrow on this earth. No one knows with absolute certainty God's timetable for this world, nor for his or her individual life. God's call on your life will no doubt come at a time when you least expect it.

Let's not dare to twist our Lord's words here to fit our so-called system of theology. The Lord meant exactly what He said. We need to *watch* our lives, to make sure we are living in the will of our Lord. There is need to be *ready* for His coming at every *hour*.

24:45-47a The position of a pastor is very opportune from the standpoint of serving the Lord. Added opportunity, of course, implies added responsibility. According to Scripture, all Christians are to be pastors to

on a day when he is not looking for him, and
at an hour in which he is not expecting him.
51 "His master will most severely punish him[a]
and assign him his proper place, with the other
hypocrites, where there will be bitter weeping
and gnashing of teeth.[b]

The Five Wise and Five Foolish

25 "At that time the Kingdom of Heaven
will be like the night when ten virgins
took their oil lamps and went out to meet the
bridegroom.
2 "Five were wise, and five were foolish.
3 "The foolish ones brought their lamps but
no extra oil.[a]
4 "While those who were wise brought along
containers with plenty of extra oil to keep their
lamps burning.
5 "But while the bridegroom delayed his
arrival, they all became drowsy and fell asleep.
6 "Then at midnight the cry rang out,
'Everybody up! Here comes the bridegroom!
Go out now to meet him!'
7 "And all those virgins got up and began to
trim the wicks of their lamps.
8 "But then the foolish ones said to the wise,
'Give us some of your oil! Our lamps are
going out!'
9 'No!' the wise ones replied, 'we may not
have enough for both you and us. Go to the
store and buy some for yourselves.'
10 "And while the foolish ones were gone,
buying oil, the bridegroom came. Those who
were ready went in with him to the wedding,
after which the door was shut.
11 "Later, the others arrived. 'Sir! Oh Sir!'
they called out. 'Open the door for us!'
12 "But he replied, 'I tell you the truth, I don't
know you.'
13 "So you must always watch,[a] because you
don't know the day nor the hour when the Son
of Man is coming.

---

each other. Each follower of Jesus is admonished to encourage and strengthen, to challenge, to rebuke, to give guidance and leadership to fellow Christians. The Lord promises rewards to all of His faithful servants who give His household *food at the proper time*. Verse 47 indicates that the rewards for faithful service will be great indeed.

24:51a Literally *will cut him in two*.

24:48-51b Some Christians, including some pastors, seem to have little concern for the fact that Christ may call them from this world at any moment to appear before Him. The one who thinks he can get by for a time with sin, later straightening himself out, will no doubt find his Lord coming for him at a time when least expected. It will pay great dividends to always *watch* and be *ready* to meet the Lord. Such a life has the reward now of peace of mind and real assurance of eternal life—and later—eternal rewards.

The *servant of the Lord* who lives in sin was either never really converted in the sense of having his life changed—being truly born again—which is the only kind of conversion recognized by the Lord (John 3:1-12; 2 Corinthians 5:17), or if converted, he somehow lost out to the temptations of the flesh and the devil. His end will come suddenly, when he is least expecting it. After this life is over, such an unfaithful servant will find his place with those who have openly opposed the Lord, and with his own kind, *the hypocrites*. These are frightful warnings indeed, coming directly from the mouth of Jesus, Himself. We will do well to take earnest heed ourselves and to shout the warnings and urge all who profess Christ as Lord and Savior to live thoroughly what they profess. These prophecies of warning are just as certain of fulfillment as the prophecies of blessing. See Mark 9:43-47 and note.

25:3a The foolish virgins are a picture of those who want and expect to get to heaven, but as cheaply as possible. The awful truth here is, they won't make it.

God demands our all—all our love, all our talents and strengths to be used for His glory and the blessing and salvation of others, and full obedience to all His teachings and commands. Anything less than total commitment is not true conversion.

25:13a Meaning, watch the way you live. It's in the present tense, imperative mood, denoting present, necessary action that must be continuous. Don't ever think you can get by with a half measure of spiritual interest and concern and still be welcomed into heaven. God demands your whole heart, full and brimming over with love for Him.

Is your life really pleasing to the Lord, or are you mainly living to please yourself and certain others, instead of the Lord? Do you truly love the Lord above all else and above all others? Are you truly born again? Are you continuing in the faith? John 8:31; I John 2:24; James 5:19-20.

* * *

This should be a frightful warning to many believers. For the foolish virgins were all followers of the Lord. That is, in a sense they were. They were waiting for the com-

The Story about Three Servants

14 "The Kingdom of Heaven is also like what happened when a man traveled to another country. Before going he called in three of his servants and entrusted each of them with some of his money to invest for him.

15 "To one he gave five talents,[a] to another two, to another one–to each man according to his ability. Then he went on his trip.

16 "The first one invested the five talents, and made another five.

17 "The one who had two did the same, and made two more.

18 "But the one who had received the one talent dug a hole in the ground and hid his master's money.

19 "After a long time the master returned home. He soon called in each servant to report what he had done with his money.

20 "So the one who had received the five talents came with them and also brought the five additional talents. 'Sir,' he said, 'you gave me five talents, and, as you see, I have gained five more, to add to the ones you gave me.'

21 'Well done!' his master replied. 'You have been a capable and faithful servant. Because you have been faithful in the handling of a few things, I will put you in charge of many things. Come on in and share my happiness!'

22 "The one who had received two talents also came. 'Sir,' he said, 'you gave me two talents, and look, I have gained two more, to add to the ones you gave me.'

23 'Well done!' his master replied. 'You have been a capable and faithful servant. Because you have been faithful in the handling of a few things, I will put you in charge of many things. Come on in and share my happiness!'

24 "Then the one who had been given one talent came. 'Sir,' he said, 'I know that you are a hard man. You reap harvests where you haven't planted, and you gather in where you haven't scattered any seed.

25 'So I was afraid,[a] and I went out and hid your talent in the ground. Look, here now you have what is yours.'

26 "But his master replied, 'You wicked, lazy servant! So you're sure you know, are you, that I reap a harvest where I haven't planted, and gather in where I haven't scattered any seed?

27 'In that case you should have at least earned honest money for me by depositing my money in the bank, so that on my return I would have received back what belonged to me, with interest.

28 'Take the talent from him,' he told his other servants, 'and give it to the one with the ten talents!

29 'Because everyone who diligently uses what he has will be given more, and he will have an abundance. As for the one who has nothing, *because of his fear and unfaithfulness*,[a] even the little he has will be taken from him.

30 'And throw the worthless servant into the outer darkness, where there will be weeping and gnashing of teeth.'[a]

---

ing of the Lord. *John Calvin* once stated, "The simple and genuine meaning of the whole of this parable is just this, that it is not enough to have a lively zeal for awhile. We must have in addition a perseverance that never tires."

The Apostle Peter warned, "Be most diligent to make your calling and election to salvation and eternal life with God a sure thing." 2 Peter 1:10. The Apostle Paul warned early believers (Acts 14:22) that they must "continue in the faith." He warned the Colossians (1:23) that they would be saved "...if in truth you continue in the faith, deeply rooted and unflinching and fixed in your direction, and not allow yourselves to be seduced and led away from the hope that came to you when you heard and accepted the Great News."

So many other warnings in Scripture could be pointed out.

* * *

What to do? "Draw near to God, and He will draw near to you." James 4:8. How? By reading your Bible daily, and obeying everything that God teaches you there. To stay alive spiritually you must read what God has to say, and obey it. Also, have a good daily visit with the Lord in prayer. In fact, have constant fellowship with Him.

Remember, the Lord promised and warned (Matthew 10:22 and 24:13) "Whoever remains true to Me to the end will be saved."

For further note on this parable, see appendix 202.

25:15a Very likely silver talents. In Israel, each talent of silver (troy weight) would weigh 1440 ounces.

25:25a ... afraid *you would rob me of anything I earned...*

25:29a Implied.

25:14-30a Jesus pictures Himself here as a *man traveling into a far country*. Before His departure He calls *His own servants* to His side. These servants are not rebels or ungodly men. They are persons in the employ of the Master. All Christians are the Lord's servants, and we all have unending,

The Judgment of the Nations

31 "When the Son of Man comes in His glory,
and all the holy angels with Him, He will sit
upon His glorious throne.
32 "Then all the people of all the nations in
the world will be gathered before Him. And
He will separate them from one another in the
same way that a shepherd separates his sheep
from the goats.
33 "He will put the sheep at His right, but the
goats at His left.
34 "Then the King will say to the people at His
right, 'Come, you who are now so accepted
and blessed by My Father, and inherit the
Kingdom that was prepared for you before the
world was created.
35 'Because I was hungry and you gave Me
food. I was thirsty and you gave Me something to drink. I was alone and away from
home, and you welcomed Me into your
homes.
36 'I needed clothes, and you gave Me something to wear. I was sick and you cared for
Me. I was in jail and you came to visit Me.'
37 "Then those who had done what was right
will say to Him, 'Lord, when did we ever see
You hungry, and give You food? Or thirsty,
and give You something to drink?
38 'When did we ever see You alone, away
from home, and invite You into our homes?
When did we see You in need of clothes, and
give You something to wear?
39 'Or when did we see You sick or in jail, and
came to visit You?'
40 "The King will reply, 'I tell you the truth,
when you did it for one of the least known or

---

serious responsibilities. God has given various gifts and opportunities to every servant. He expects each servant to use these talents, material means, open doors, and every other means at hand for the furtherance of His message of salvation to a lost world.

To some, God has entrusted great natural capabilities or financial means. Others have lesser abilities or financial means. Whether limited to one talent or granted a large number of talents, all servants will *appear before the judgment seat of Christ*. 2 Corinthians 5:10. And from this parable we are forewarned that this appearing will be a most serious matter. It will be a time of great rejoicing for those who have been faithful. But for the one who has been slothful, constantly giving excuses for not having served the Lord with zeal, to such it will be a day of frightful awakening.

* * *

Though we are not saved by our works, good works in obedience to the Lord's commands must accompany faith, or that faith is counterfeit. It's a joy to think of the two servants here who were found faithful, and were commended by their master and welcomed into His presence to great responsibilities, opportunities, and happiness. What joy to be found among the number who have been faithful in *serving the Lord* in the home, the factory, the school, the office, the church, the neighborhood, and wherever else the opportunity has been afforded!

But the task of calling attention to the unfaithful servant is not a pleasant one. We would rather not speak of him. We would rather not think that any such thing could happen to one of the Lord's *own servants*. We see that his final end is to be cast *into outer darkness*. No, this was not a hypocrite, as such. He was just *slothful* and *fearful*. Yes, I guess you would have to call him a hypocrite of some sort.

* * *

It would appear that the person to whom God has given but *one talent* has the greatest opportunity of all to show himself faithful to his Lord. If you can use that one talent in such a way that it will be a great blessing and joy to your Lord, as well as to your fellow Christians and the unsaved, you can stand before the Lord with confidence. And your Master will reward you with a large place of opportunity, responsibility, and joy in His Kingdom.

Let no one say that he cannot do anything for the Lord. Most Christians can read and study God's Word, at least, seeking to know the Master's will, that they might *obey* Him. In the second place, our Lord created us for fellowship and communion with Himself. We can bring joy to our Lord by the times we spend with Him in prayer and praise, rejoicing that it is our privilege to be in His presence by this means for now, and later on to see Him face to face. Every Christian also has opportunity to take his stand for the Lord in various situations. A Christian can witness to the lost simply by opening his mouth and asking, "Are you planning on making it to heaven?" The response to that question will give you the clue as to what to say next. There is no learning how to witness unless a person starts somehow, somewhere.

* * *

Remember, this servant had not abused or misused his talent; he had simply not put it to work for his master, as his master had ordered him.

least important of My brothers or sisters, you
were doing it for Me.'
41 "Then the King will give vent to those at
His left and declare, 'Out of My presence, you
detestable ones! Away with you into the everlasting fire[a] prepared for the devil and his
demons!
42 'Because I was hungry, but you would not
feed Me. I was thirsty, but you would not give
Me a drink.
43 'I was alone and away from home, but you
wouldn't welcome Me into your homes. I
needed clothes, but you wouldn't give Me anything to wear. I was sick, and in jail, but you
didn't visit Me.'
44 "Then they also will ask Him, 'Lord, when
did we ever see You hungry or thirsty or alone
and away from home or in need of clothes or
sick or in jail, and refused to help You?'
45 "Then He will reply, 'I tell you the truth,
anything you refused to do for one of these
people of Mine, even for the least important
one, you refused to do for Me.'
46 "These will go away into everlasting punishment, but those who lived lives pleasing to
God will enter everlasting life."[a]

The Plot to Kill Jesus

26 When Jesus had finished giving all of
these parables and prophecies, He said
to His followers,
2 "As you know, the Passover celebration
begins two days from now. And that's when
the Son of Man will be turned over to the
Romans to be nailed to a cross."[a]
3 In fact, at that very moment the chief
priests, the teachers of the Law, and the elders
of the people were assembled in the palace of
Caiaphas the High Priest.
4 They were discussing ways and means of
arresting Jesus in some underhanded way and
killing Him.

"Spiritual indolence (inaction) is as serious a sin as active wickedness, and meets with similar punishment." So said one of God's servants of the 19th century. His reference for the statement was this very Scripture. It would be profitable for whoever names the name of Christ as Lord and Savior to give very serious consideration to our Lord's prophecy here concerning His servants. When a person is honestly born again, Jesus is Lord in that life. When He is actually Lord, the servant is quite willing and anxious to take orders from Him. Most of those orders are to be found in His Word.

May the day of His appearing be a crowning day for you. For additional comments on this parable see Appendix 203.

25:41a Matthew 13:41-42; Luke 16:19-31; Revelation 14:9-11; 20:10-15.

25:46a The account here of God's judgment is not a full account of details, but it gives an indication of the criterion which will govern the verdicts.

Some believe this is a judgment of those who will still be alive on earth after the great wars and tribulation of the end time. God's people will have gone to meet Christ in the air as He is returning. I Thessalonians 4:16-17; Matthew 24:29-31. So they will not be included in this judgment. Those declared righteous here are *not* said to inherit the Kingdom of heaven. They will be the people who will be the citizens of God's new kingdom on earth.

They are the people who have shown mercy to God's people (both Christians and Jews) who were persecuted by Antichrist during the last three-and-a-half years of this age. Read Daniel, chapters 7,8,11,12, and especially verses 7:9-11,18,21-22,25; 8:24; 11:32-34; 12:7. These verses tell of the great conflict that will rage between God's people and the Antichrist in the last years of the age. The accounts in these verses are not in sequence, but as you read them all you will begin to see the picture. We suggest that you underline these verses in your Bible, or highlight them, and that you read them over several times.

* * *

The kind of everlasting life these righteous ones will experience on earth is not explained, but the punishment given those who showed no mercy will no doubt be the same hell that all who opposed and ignored God throughout the ages will experience.

This does not mean that those already with Christ at this time did not need to extend mercy to others to be saved. If they were truly born again they were people who lived to please God in every way. And one indication that a person is truly born again is that he is concerned about the needs of others (both physical and spiritual needs), and does something about it. Matthew 5:7; 6:12-15; 18:23-35.

Always remember, *When you help the poor (both the physically and spiritually poor), you are lending to the Lord, and it's the Lord who will repay you.* Proverbs 19:17.

For further note on this judgment, see Appendix 204.

26:2a Crucified.

5 "But we can't do it during Passover," they
said, "or the people may riot."

Jesus Honored at Bethany

6 While Jesus was in Bethany at the home of
Simon, a former leper,
7 a woman came to Him with an alabaster jar
of very expensive perfume. She proceeded to
pour it on His head as He reclined at the
table.[a]
8 When Jesus' followers saw what she was
doing, they became angry, and said, "Why this
waste?
9 "That perfume could have been sold for a
fabulous price, and the money given to the
poor!"
10 But Jesus, knowing what they were saying,
said, "Why are you giving this woman a hard
time? What she has just done for Me was a
beautiful thing.
11 "You will always have the poor with you,
but you won't always have Me.
12 "When she poured this perfume on Me,
she was preparing My body for burial.
13 "I tell you the truth, wherever the Great
News is preached throughout the whole world,
what this woman has done will also be told, as
a memorial to her."

A Traitor Negotiates to Betray Jesus

14 Then Judas Iscariot, one of the Twelve,
went to the chief priests.
15 "What are you willing to pay me if I hand
Jesus over to you?" he asked them. And they
counted out thirty silver coins and gave them
to him.
16 So from that time on Judas looked for a
chance to hand Him over to them.

Jesus Eats Last Passover Meal with His Followers

17 On the first day of the Feast of Unleavened
Bread, Jesus' followers went to Him and
asked, "Where do you want us to prepare for
You to eat the Passover meal?"
18 He mentioned the name of a certain man,
and said, "Go into the city and tell him, 'The
Teacher says, "My time is drawing near. My
followers and I will eat the Passover meal in
your home."'"
19 So His followers did as Jesus had instructed
them, and prepared the Passover meal there.
20 When evening came He reclined at the
table with the Twelve.
21 And as they were eating, He said, "I tell
you the truth, one of you will hand Me over to
My enemies."
22 The men were horrified and cut to the heart
upon hearing such an announcement. And
one after the other they asked Him, "Lord, You
surely don't mean me, do You?"
23 "The one who has dipped his bread in the
same bowl with Me is the one who will betray
Me,"[a] Jesus replied.
24 "The Son of Man will indeed go from this
life in the very way it has been written in
prophecy concerning His suffering and death.[a]
But awful judgment awaits the man who is
betraying the Son of Man. It would have been
better for him if he had never been born."
25 Then Judas, who was in the very process of
betraying Him, said, "Surely, Teacher, You're
not speaking of me, are You?"
"Yes, I am," Jesus replied.

Jesus Institutes the Lord's Supper

26 As they were eating, Jesus took some bread
in His hands, and after thanking God for it and
asking Him to bless it, He broke it and gave it
to His followers. "Take this and eat it," He
said. "This is My body."[a]
27 Then He took the cup, and after giving
thanks to God He handed it to them, saying,
"Drink from it, all of you.
28 "Because this is My blood[a]—the blood that
guarantees and makes possible God's New
Agreement with mankind.[b] It is being poured
out so that many may have their sins forgiven.
29 "But as for me, I will never again drink this
fruit of the vine until that day when I drink the
new wine with you in My Father's Kingdom."
30 After they sang a hymn, they went out to
the Mount of Olives.

Peter's Denial Predicted by Jesus

31 Then Jesus said to them, "Tonight you will
all be ashamed of Me and desert Me, because

26:7a The custom was to recline on couches while eating. John 12:3 states that she poured the perfume on His feet. She no doubt did both, as John 12:3 indicates she had a large amount.
26:23a According to John 13:21-26, Jesus evidently said this privately to John.
26:24a Psalm 22:1-22; 41:9; Isaiah 52:14; 53; Daniel 9:26; Zechariah 12:10; Luke 24:25-27,45-47.
26:26a Meaning *this represents* or *is a picture of* or *will bring to your remembrance* My body, which was sacrificed for you.
26:28a Meaning *this represents My blood.*
26:28b The blood that seals the new declaration of God's will, purpose, and set of

it is written:
'I will strike down the Shepherd, and the
sheep of the flock will be scattered.'[a]
32 "But after I have come back to life again, I
will go ahead of you into Galilee."
33 Then Peter spoke up and said, "Even if
everyone else loses faith in You and leaves, I
never will!"
34 "I tell you the truth," Jesus replied, "this
very night, before the rooster crows at dawn,
you will have said three times that you don't
even know Me."
35 But Peter emphatically declared, "There's
no way that I would ever deny You, even if I
must die with You!" And all the other followers said the same.

Jesus Prays in Gethsemane

36 Then Jesus went with them to a place called
Gethsemane. "Sit here," He said, "while I go
on a little farther and pray."
37 Taking with Him Peter and the two brothers, James and John, He became overwhelmed
with grief and was deeply depressed.
38 "I am extremely overwhelmed with sorrow," He said to those with Him, "so much so
that I'm at the brink of death. You must stay
here and keep watch with Me."
39 Then He went a little farther and fell with
His face to the ground, and prayed, "O My
Father, if there is any way possible, let this cup
be taken from Me![a] But still, I don't want what
I desire, but whatever You know must be
done."
40 Then He went back to His three followers—
and they were asleep! To Peter He said, "Is
this the way you stand with Me as you
promised? Couldn't you men keep watch with
Me for even one hour?
41 "You must continue to be alert, and earnestly pray, so that when temptation comes you
won't be overcome by it and fall.[a] It's true that
your spirit wants to do what's right, but the
flesh is weak!"
42 Then He left them and prayed a second
time, saying, "O My Father! If it's not possible
for this cup to be taken away unless I drink it,
Your will be done."
43 Then He came back and found them asleep
again. They just couldn't keep their heavy
eyes open.
44 So He left them again and went back and
prayed a third time, saying the same words.
45 Returning to His followers, He said, "Are
you still sleeping? Still taking your rest? But
look, the time has come! The Son of Man is
right now being betrayed into the hands of sinners.
46 "Get up now, and let's be on our way.
Look! Here comes the man who is betraying
Me!"

Betrayal and Arrest of Jesus

47 And while He was still speaking, there
came Judas, one of the Twelve, with a whole
mob of people carrying swords and clubs.
They'd been sent by the chief priests and
elders of the people.
48 Judas had prearranged a signal, saying,
"The one I greet with a kiss is the man you
want. Arrest him!"
49 He immediately went right up to Jesus and
said, "Greetings, Teacher!" and embracing
Him, kissed Him on the cheek.
50 "My friend," Jesus responded, "why all the
pretence?" Then the men with Judas came forward and grabbed Him and arrested Him.
51 But suddenly, one of Jesus' followers
pulled out his sword and slashed out at one of
the servants of the High Priest, and cut off one
of his ears.
52 "Put your sword back in its place," Jesus
told him. "Because all who use the sword will
die by the sword.
53 "Don't you realize I could call My Father
for help? If I did He would send Me more than
twelve legions[a] of angels.
54 "But if I did, how could the Scriptures be
fulfilled, that state that this is what must happen?"[a]
55 Then Jesus spoke to the mob, "Do you consider Me so dangerous that you needed to
come out against Me as you would against a
thief, with swords and clubs to take Me into
custody? I sat with you in the temple area
many days as I taught, and you didn't arrest
Me then.
56 "But all of this has happened so that the
writings of the prophets[a] might be fulfilled." It
was at this turn of events that all of His followers deserted Him and ran.

Jesus' Trial Before the Sanhedrin

57 Then those who had arrested Jesus led Him

---

regulations—the New Testament.
26:31a Zechariah 13:7.
26:39a See Mark 14:35 note.
26:41a Or *so that you won't be tempted* to lose faith in Jesus when He dies.
26:53a A Roman legion equaled more than 6,000 men.
26:54,56a See v 24 refs.

away to the home of Caiaphas, the High Priest, where all the Pharisees and teachers of the Law had gathered.
58 But far behind was Peter, following Jesus to the High Priest's courtyard. He went in and sat with the soldiers to see what would happen.
59 The chief priests, the elders, and the entire Council kept trying to find someone who could convincingly give false testimony of some wrong Jesus had done, so they could have Him put to death.
60 But they couldn't find any. Even though many false witnesses came forward, they couldn't find any whose testimony would make sure He would be put to death.
61 Finally two men came forward and said, "This fellow claimed He could destroy the temple of God and then rebuild it in three days.'"
62 The High Priest then got up and addressed Jesus, "Well, do you have an answer? Have you anything at all to say about these charges against you?"
63 But Jesus didn't say a word. Then the High Priest challenged Him, "I command you in the name of the living God that you tell us if you are indeed the Messiah, the Son of God!"
64 "Yes, it is as you say," Jesus replied. "But I will also inform you that in time to come you will see the Son of Man both sitting at the right hand of the Almighty, and coming back to earth on the clouds of heaven."
65 When the High Priest heard this he tore his clothes and shouted, "He has spoken blasphemy! What further need do we have of witnesses? Look! You all heard his blasphemy! What is your verdict?"
66 "He must die!" the crowd thundered back.
67 Then they spit in His face and pounded Him with their fists.
68 Others slapped Him with the palms of their hands, and then jeered, "Prophesy, you messiah! Who hit you that time?"

Peter's Denial of Jesus

69 Meanwhile, Peter was sitting outside in the courtyard when a servant girl came up to him and said, "You were also with Jesus, the Galilean."
70 But he denied it in front of everyone there. "I don't know what you're talking about!" he said.
71 When he went out near the gate, another girl saw him and said to those who were there, "This man was also with Jesus from Nazareth."
72 But again he denied it, this time with an oath, declaring, "I tell you, I haven't even met the man!"
73 After a short while the men standing nearby went up to Peter and said, "You have got to be one of His followers, because even your accent is proof that you're from Galilee."
74 At this he began to curse. Then he declared, "I swear to God, as I told you, I haven't even met the man!" And immediately a rooster crowed.
75 Then Peter remembered that Jesus had told him: "Before the rooster crows at dawn, you will say three times that you don't even know Me." And he went out and cried bitterly.

A Hurry-Up Early Morning Trial

27 Very early that morning, all the chief priests and elders of the people met together to decide what steps should be taken to make sure that Jesus was put to death.
2 Then after tying Him up,[a] they led Him away and turned Him over to Pontius Pilate, the governor.

The Traitor Hangs Himself

3 When Judas, the traitor, saw that Jesus had been sentenced to death, he was extremely sorry for what he had done, and brought the thirty silver coins back to the chief priests and elders.
4 "I have sinned by betraying a man who never did anything wrong!" he blurted out.
"That has nothing to do with us," they sneered. "That's your problem."
5 Judas then violently hurled the silver coins to the floor of the temple, and left, and went off and hanged himself.
6 As the chief priests picked up the coins, they said, "It would be against our Law to put this money back into the treasury, because it's blood money."
7 After considering the matter they decided to use the money to buy the field from which the potter had dug his clay, as a place to bury strangers.
8 So to this very day that field is called the Field of Blood.
9 This fulfilled what Jeremiah the prophet had prophesied, when he said:

> "And they took the thirty silver coins, the amount they had been willing to pay for Him (this was the miserable value placed on Him by the sons of Israel)
> 10 and gave them in payment for the potter's field, as that's what the Lord had told me to do."[a]

27:2a This possibly consisted only in tying His hands together.

27:10a Zechariah 11:12-13.

Pilate Questions Jesus

11 Meanwhile, Jesus stood before the governor. "Are you the King of the Jews?" the governor asked Him.
"Yes, what you say is true," Jesus replied.
12 And yet, while He was being accused by
the chief priests and elders, He gave them no
answer.
13 "Don't you hear all the charges they are
making against you?" Pilate demanded.
14 But Jesus didn't say even one word in
answer to his question, which utterly amazed
the governor.

Jesus is Sentenced to Death

15 Now it was the custom during Passover for
the governor to free whichever Jewish prisoner
the people wanted freed.
16 At that time a well-known rebel named
Barabbas was in jail.
17 So when a crowd had gathered, Pilate
asked the people, "Whom do you want me to
release to you—Barabbas, or Jesus, who is
called the Messiah?"
18 He said this because he knew very well that
the Jewish leaders had turned Jesus over to him
because they were jealous of Him.
19 But just then, as Pilate was sitting on the
judge's bench, his wife sent him a note, saying,
"Don't have anything to do with condemning
this good man, because I went through extreme
suffering last night in a dream about Him."
20 Meanwhile, as Pilate was receiving the
note and reading it, the chief priests and elders
were convincing the crowd to ask for the
release of Barabbas and to have Jesus put to
death.
21 So when Pilate again asked, "Which of the
two do you want me to release to you?" the
crowd shouted back,
"Barabbas!"
22 "What should I do, then, with Jesus, who is
called the Messiah?" Pilate asked.
"Crucify[a] him!" they all shouted.
23 "Why?" the governor demanded. "What
wrong has He done?" But the crowd just kept
shouting, even louder, "Crucify him! Crucify[a]
him!"
24 When Pilate realized he was getting
nowhere with them, but that instead he was
about to have a riot on his hands, he took a
basin of water and washed His hands[a] in front
of the crowd, saying, "I refuse to have anything to do with killing this innocent man. It's
now up to you what you do with him."
25 "Yes, you can place the blame for His
bloody death on us and on our children!"
someone shouted. And that whole mob shouted their agreement.
26 So he released Barabbas to them. But he
ordered that Jesus be whipped,[a] after which he
turned Him over to the soldiers to be crucified.

The Soldiers Scornfully Insult Jesus

27 The governor's soldiers then took Jesus
into the Praetorium, where all the soldiers of
the entire garrison gathered around Him.
28 First they took off His clothes and put a
bright red robe on Him.
29 After twisting some thorn branches with
long, sharp thorns, into a crown, they put it on
His head. Then in mockery they put a slender
pole in His right hand as a scepter. In further
mockery they knelt before Him and shouted,
"Hail! King of the Jews!"
30 After repeatedly spitting on Him, they
grabbed the pole out of His hand and beat Him
on the head with it again and again.[a]
31 After they got tired of mocking Him, they
took the red robe off Him and put His own
clothes back on, and then led Him away to be
crucified.

The Crucifixion

32 On the way they met a man from Cyrene,
in Libya, named Simon. The soldiers forced
him to carry Jesus' cross.
33 When they came to the place called
Golgotha, which means *The Place That
Looks Like a Skull*,
34 they gave Jesus vinegar wine to drink,
mixed with a drug to ease the pain. But when
Jesus tasted what it was, He refused to drink it.
35 Then they nailed Him to a cross. And as
He hung there they divided His clothing
among them and threw dice for His robe, thus
fulfilling David's prophecy:
"They divided My clothing among them and
threw dice for My robe."[a]
36 Then they sat down, to keep guard over

27:22,23a Meaning *Nail him to a cross*!

27:24a He was symbolizing that he was washing his hands of the whole affair. He was a man in a responsible position who refused to take responsible action, thinking he could absolve himself of responsibility by his inaction. There's a lesson here for each of us, as well.

27:26a See John 19:1 note.

27:30a ... *driving the long thorns ever painfully deeper into His skull.*

27:35a Psalm 22:18. See John 19:23-24.

Him.[a]
37 Above His head they had placed a written
notice of the charge against Him, which read:

THIS IS JESUS
THE KING OF THE JEWS

38 They had also nailed two robbers on cross-
es, one on each side of Jesus.
39 And the people passing by kept shaking
their heads and hurling vicious insults at Him.
40 "So you're the one who could destroy the
temple and rebuild it in three days!" they shouted. "If you're the Son of God, save yourself
now and come down from the cross!"
41 The chief priests, elders, and teachers of the
Law were ridiculing Him in the same vile way.
42 "He saved others," they shouted, "but He
can't save himself! If He's the King of Israel, as
He claims, let him come down now from the
cross, and we'll believe him.
43 "He says He trusts in God. Well, let God
deliver him now if He wants him. After all, He
claims, 'I am the Son of God!'"
44 Even the robbers who were crucified with
Him threw the same insults at Him.

The Death of Jesus

45 Then at noon a most amazing thing happened. The whole country became enveloped
in darkness, a condition which lasted until three
in the afternoon!
46 It was about three o'clock when Jesus cried
out with a loud voice, "Eli! Eli! lama
sabachthani?" which means, "My God! My
God! why have You abandoned Me?"[a]
47 When some of the people standing there
heard Him, they said, "The man's calling for
Elijah!"
48 Immediately one of them ran and got a
sponge, filled it with vinegar wine, put it on a
stick, and lifted it up for Him to drink.
49 But the rest of them said, "Leave him alone!
Let's see if Elijah really will come and save
him."
50 When Jesus had cried out again with a loud
voice, He yielded up His spirit and died.
51 Immediately, there was a great earthquake!
Rocks split apart, and the great curtain in the
temple separating the Holy Place from the Most
Holy Place was torn in two from top to
bottom![a]
52 Tombs broke open, and the bodies of many
godly people who had died came back to life.
53 After Jesus' resurrection these people then
left the cemetery and went into Jerusalem,
where many people saw them.
54 When the captain, and the soldiers who
were with him guarding Jesus, felt the severe
earthquake and saw everything else that happened, they were extremely shocked, and said,
"Without a doubt, this Man really was the Son
of God!"
55 Many women who had come with Jesus
from Galilee to be of help to Him were there,
watching from a distance.
56 Among them were Mary Magdalene, Mary
the mother of James and Joses, and the mother
of James and John.

Jesus Buried in Joseph's Tomb

57 In the late afternoon, Joseph, a rich man
from Arimathea who had also become a follower of Jesus,
58 went to Pilate and asked for Jesus' body.
And Pilate ordered that it be given to him.
59 After taking the body down, Joseph
wrapped it in a clean linen cloth.
60 Then he laid it in his own new tomb that he
had carved out of a wall of rock, and rolled a
large stone in front of its entrance, and left.
61 Mary Magdalene and the other Mary had
been there, sitting across from the tomb, watching.

The Tomb Sealed and Guarded

62 The next day, the day after the Sabbath
preparations, the chief priests and Pharisees
went together to see Pilate.
63 "Sir," they said, "we remember what that
deceiver said while he was alive. He declared,
'After three days I will come back to life again.'
64 "So please order the tomb to be securely
sealed and carefully guarded until after the third
day. Otherwise, His followers may come at
night, steal His body, and then announce to the
people that He has risen from the dead. In that
event the last deception would be worse than
the first."
65 "Your request for a guard is granted," Pilate
replied. "Go and make it as secure as you can."
66 So they left, and secured the tomb by
putting a seal on the stone and leaving soldiers
to watch it.

The Resurrection

28 After the Sabbath days[a] had ended, and
as Sunday morning began to dawn,

27:36a ... *to make sure no one would come and take Him down.*
27:46a Psalm 22:1.
27:51a Regarding the *great curtain,* see Luke 23:45 note.
28:1a There were evidently two Sabbath

Mary Magdalene and the other Mary went to
see the tomb.
2 Suddenly there was a violent earthquake,
caused by an angel of the Lord who came
down from heaven and rolled the stone away
from the door of the tomb, and then sat on it.
3 His appearance was as brilliant and striking
as lightning. And his clothes were as white as
snow.
4 The soldiers guarding the tomb were so
shaken up with fear when they saw him, that
they fainted and appeared to be dead.
5 But the angel spoke to the women. "Don't
be afraid," he said. "I know you are looking
for Jesus, who was crucified.
6 "But He is not here, because He has risen
from the dead, just as He said He would. Come
on in and see the place where He was lying.
7 "Now run and tell His followers that He is
risen from the dead, and is going ahead of you
into Galilee. You will see Him there. Now I have
told you the message I was sent to give you."
8 So they immediately left the tomb, after
being badly frightened, but also now filled with
great joy! And they ran to bring the news to
His followers.
9 But as they were on their way—suddenly,
Jesus, Himself, met them. "Rejoice!" He said.
Dropping to their knees, they held Him by
His feet and worshiped Him.
10 Then Jesus spoke to them. "Don't be
afraid. But go and tell My brothers to go to
Galilee, and they will see Me there."

The Guards Agree to Lie

11 While they were on their way, some of the
soldiers who had been guarding the tomb went
into the city and reported to the chief priests all
that had happened.
12 When the chief priests had gotten together
with the elders, and had considered the matter,
they gave the soldiers a large sum of money.
13 "You are to say," they were told, 'His followers came at night and stole him away while
we were asleep.'
14 "If the governor hears about your sleeping,
we'll pacify him somehow, and keep you out
of trouble."
15 So they took the money and did as they
were told. And the report they spread is the
report that's being spread among the Jews to
this very day.

The Great Commission

16 Then the eleven followers went to Galilee, to
the mountain where Jesus had told them to go.
17 When they saw Him, they worshiped Him.
But some still couldn't believe it was really Jesus.
18 Then Jesus came over to them and said,
"Unlimited power has been given to Me[a] in
heaven and on earth.
19 "I want you to go to everyone in every
nation and teach them to follow Me.[a] Baptize
them in the name of the Father and of the Son

---

days here. This would be needful if Christ was to be dead three days and three nights, as He prophesied. And the word Sabbath here is plural in the Greek text.

God had commanded that several special Sabbaths be observed each year in Israel, in addition to the regular Sabbaths. The Day of Atonement, the 10th day of the 7th month, was a special Sabbath. Leviticus 16:29-31; 23:26-32. The Feast of Trumpets, the 1st day of the 7th month, was a special Sabbath. Leviticus 23:23-25.

The Passover was observed after sundown on the 14th day of the first Israeli month (Nisan). Leviticus 23:5. The very next day, the 15th of Nisan, was always a special Sabbath. That was the first day of the Feast of Unleavened Bread. It was an extra Sabbath they were commanded to observe. Leviticus 23:6-7.

So what evidently happened was that Jesus ate the Passover in the beginning hours of the 14th of Nisan, as the Jewish day begins at sundown. At three o'clock in the afternoon of the same day, He (the Lamb of God) died on the cross. He must have been crucified on a Thursday. The special Sabbath (the first day of the Feast of Unleavened Bread), the 15th of Nisan, was the next day (Friday). That was then followed by the regular Sabbath, making the two Sabbaths, resulting in Jesus being dead parts of three days and three whole nights.

Mention is made in John 19:31 that this Sabbath was a *special* Sabbath.

And further proof that Jesus died on Thursday: The Sunday afternoon after the crucifixion as two of Jesus' followers were on their way to Emmaus, they stated that it *had now been three days since Jesus died*. Luke 24:21. If He had died on Friday it would have been only two days since He died.

28:18a ... *by My Father*, ...

28:19a This commission now becomes ours to fulfill—to reach everyone in our time. To be righteous we must do everything that God calls us to do. Although we cannot achieve perfection in this obedience, it must nevertheless be our sincere intention and supreme aim to do so.

and of the Holy Spirit.[b]
20 "And teach them to obey everything that I have commanded you.[a] And listen! I will always be with you, even to the very end of the age."[b] So be it!

28:19b Mark 16:15-16

28:20a Keeping His commandments is not optional for those who desire to inherit eternal life. It is an essential aspect of saving faith. There is no saving faith apart from obedience. Romans 2:1-10; 6:16; Hebrews 5:9. The obedience of even the most godly Christian will be imperfect; but even though imperfect, the intention to fully obey must nevertheless be real. Luke 6:46-49; John 3:36; 14:21-23; 15:8-10, 13-14; James 1:22; 2 Peter 1:8-11; 1 John 2:3-5.

28:18-20b These three verses contain what is called the Great Commission. This commission was not given only to the eleven followers of Christ. They are not living now, so they could not be reaching out to those who are alive today. The Commission is to all of Christ's followers. We are all to be missionaries. All of us are to be reaching out to those who still need to hear the Great News. If we are truly born again we will be reaching out to others. See Romans 10:9-10.

God was so concerned about our lost condition that He sent His Son in the person of Jesus Christ to suffer and die for our sins. And Jesus was so concerned that He was willing to come from heaven to be our Savior. We must likewise be intensely concerned for those who are still lost and need the message of God's love. Without God's forgiveness their future is a tragic and terrible one. Therefore, we are responsible to go to them with what we know, and learn everything else we can so that we will have the message of life to give them.

He's With Us — With Power

Then notice that Jesus informs us that He has been given unlimited power by the Father. And in the last part of this commission He promises that He will always be with us. He will always be with us with unlimited power! With such promises we should be willing to go forth boldly, knowing that we have Jesus with us and that He has all power necessary to make it possible for us to effectively witness to those who are still lost.

And notice that the command is that we teach these new converts to obey *everything* that Jesus commanded His apostles to obey. Christ's message is still in force today. His commands are just as binding upon us today as they were upon the apostles.

Also, each convert is to be baptized in the name of the Father, Son, and Holy Spirit.

Don't lightly regard these commands from the Lord. It is the responsibility of every one of us to go to others with the message of life. Just a few suggestions: It is not necessary to try to move the conversation around to spiritual things in order to talk to people about the Lord. Many times the best way is to just break right into a conversation and ask the question, "Say, are you planning on making it to heaven?" Or, "Do you know how to get to heaven—for sure?" Or even ask the question, "How does your future look?" Another question you could ask is, "What do you think of Jesus Christ?"

The hardest part about witnessing for Jesus is getting started. Any one of these questions, or some other question, will enable you to get started in the conversation. Once the door is opened you can talk to that person about his or her need. Don't wait for opportunities to witness, make opportunities! And you can make opportunities by asking such questions. If you find it impossible to begin witnessing, apply James 5:16 here. "The fervent, persevering prayer of a person who is right with God is powerfully effective, and accomplishes great things." Go to God in desperation and in fervent prayer, and He will help you and fill you with His Spirit, who has been sent for this very purpose. Luke 11:13

Granted, it is not always wise to use the bold approach. With neighbors, friends, relatives, etc. it is wise to use what is called Friendship Evangelism. Your very life should and must be a witness. Don't hide the light you have; let it shine, by your love for them, and by the things you say and do. But there comes a time when you must speak out for the Lord if the subject has not come up naturally.

On the other hand there are the many you come into contact with whom you may never see again.

These are the ones you need to speak out to boldly. You may be the only one who will ever speak to them about their need. Don't fail them. And don't fail the Lord.

Don't Worry

Don't worry about questions or arguments that may come up for which you have no answers. Let those questions come up, and then somehow find the answer. Someone will have the answer for you, or God in some special way will bring the answer to you. Then the next time that question or argument comes up you will have the answer. The more you witness, the more answers you will have. You learn by doing. So we can all be missionaries right where we are, wherever that may be. Begin now to obey Christ by witnessing to everyone possible! The day of reckoning will soon be here. Will you be found faithful?

Find good printed material that you can leave with those to whom you witness. In that way you will have a continuing contact with them as they read what you left them. Getting them to read the Bible or the New testament will be the greatest material you can get them to read.

See Appendixes 212 and 226 for further help and instructions about witnessing.

Appendixes

200 Matthew 5:12

Do lukewarm "Christians" and unbelievers speak well of you? If so read what Christ had to say about you in Luke 6:26.

To be like the prophets of old, from the distant past to the recent past, is to be outspoken (as Christ and His apostles were) and to teach what they taught! There are so many these days who are called "a really nice guy" who preach a watered-down, easy way to heaven. They are a stench and a disgrace to Christianity! You cannot be like them and expect a great reward in heaven. They want their rewards now, and that's all they will have. Matthew 16:24-27.

Jesus taught that the way to heaven is *difficult*. Matthew 7:14. Be like Christ, and like His faithful servants of the past who have faithfully preached the whole message of the New Testament, without compromise. Christ doesn't promise popularity in the present life when you do, but He does promise a GREAT REWARD in heaven.

Live and speak out boldly for God right where you are, and there's no telling what the final great results will be. Never feel sorry for yourself under persecution, but rejoice–leap for joy! Your future is great! Jesus guarantees it.

200A Matthew 7:14

Just what is the narrow gate that leads to everlasting life? In John 10:7-9 Jesus states that He is the door and the gate that leads to life. What does He mean by that? First of all, He means that because of your sin, He, God's incomparable Son, and your Creator (John 1:2-4), became man, and died on the cross to make it possible for God to forgive your sin. But He also means that He is the Lord whom we must now obey if we are to gain life. See Romans 6:16; Hebrews 5:9. So the key that now opens the gate for you to enter eternal life is your acknowledgment that Jesus Christ is your Savior, and that you will from now on, with God's help, obey Him as your Lord. Romans 10:9-10.

The narrow gate gets us started on the right road. But also, the road that leads to eternal life is narrow and hazardous. There are all kinds of temptations along the way that must be overcome. There are tests of obedience that you will constantly meet up with. It's not easy to triumph over natural inclinations day by day. Another time (Luke 13:24) Jesus said, "You must use extreme effort in order to gain entrance through the narrow gate." And the same is true as you walk the path that leads to life. It's easy enough to believe and to accept the fact that Jesus is the Savior, but to truly obey Him as Lord is difficult indeed.

* * *

The extreme effort needed to enter the gate that leads to heaven involves determination to overcome (Revelation 2 & 3) with God's help, the various sins of the flesh, and all other sins with which Satan has you enslaved to himself. He is passionately anti-God, and he doesn't want you to become a child of God and inherit heaven. He will do everything in his power to keep you from making the decision in the first place to enthrone Jesus in your life as Lord. And once you enter the gate that leads to life, Satan will do his dead-level-best to trip you up, and get you to leave the path to heaven. But Jesus has promised to be with you (Revelation 3:20-21; John 14:23; Philippians 2:12-13) to help you overcome. With His help you will safely arrive home in heaven!

But until you have entered the narrow gate in truth, you are not on the way to life at all. No one becomes a follower of the Lord without first counting the cost. But you must also consider the awful cost of not becoming a follower. The way to heaven is not an easy way, but it's a most rewarding way. There's no middle road. No lukewarmness is accepted by God. Revelation 3:15-16. There's no fence to straddle, to keep from being on either of the roads. You're already on one of them. The path to life is rough, steep, and hedged in on both sides, because in the will of God we must crucify evil passions–we must forgo many pleasures and activities, especially if Christ would have no part in them.

You must be willing to let some of life's prizes go by. You're living for much higher and unsurpassed eternal prizes. You must be willing to part with much of what the world calls success. You are called to take up your cross and follow in the footsteps of your Lord. See notes on Matthew 10:38 and Mark 8:34-38.

* * *

As a wise person is willing to do without many things as He devotes himself to his education in preparation for a short and uncertain future after that of possibly sixty or seventy years, how much wiser it is to be willing to suffer the loss of even all things (if necessary), for the next sixty or seventy years, in order to make certain that your endless eternal future will be rich and fulfilling. So much is at stake!

"He is no fool who gives up what he cannot keep to gain what he cannot lose."

As the next verses in Matthew warn, beware of false teachers! They are everywhere. They are preaching an easy way to heaven, which will never get you there. They are agents of Satan. If a minister's message doesn't go all the way with Christ's teachings, do not believe him. Believe what Christ and his apostles taught, and you will be safe.

* * *

But don't ever think that the Christian life is a cheerless life. No, it's a thrilling, challenging, and fulfilling life. It's a real challenge to live for Christ, and speak out for Him, especially when we have the promise from Him that He will always be with us. Matthew 20:18-20. He has also promised He will always be at our side to help us to overcome every temptation and trial. See Philippians 2:12-13, and the note there. See also 1 Corinthians 10:13; 1 Peter 1:15; Hebrews 12:1-2; John 15:1-5.

And just like going on a trip, part of the joy of the Christian life is anticipating the joys, riches and total fulfillment ahead at the end of the road. You may be a pilgrim as you walk the narrow road, but a crown awaits those who overcome. Christ never promised that the Christian life would be easy, but He has promised that the results in an endless eternity will be glorious indeed! ***You cannot afford not to enter the narrow gate and then walk the narrow way with resolute, unflinching, and zealous determination!***

200B Matthew 7:23

The present tense here indicates that they are fresh from the scenes and acts of their disobedience. Those who pick and choose the commandments in the New Testament that they are willing to obey, and who disregard (thereby disobey) the rest, are living in blatant disobedience to God! According to this warning from Christ, they will be barred from heaven. Therefore if this applies to you, repent, and make absolutely sure that you are genuinely born again. 2 Peter 1:10. Also, remember, God won't accept *work* for *obedience*. Teaching, preaching and active zeal for Christ are no guarantee that you are living in obedience to Him in other matters, or that you are teaching others the absolute necessity of obedience. Read your Bible to know what God would have you do. Then do it, no matter what the cost. Your very life depends on it!

These words of Christ are indeed future prophecy. They are prophecies of warning, that only the rebellious will ignore or regard lightly. As we will point out several times in these notes: The obedience of even the most godly Christian will be imperfect; but even though imperfect, the intent to fully obey God must be real.

200C Matthew 7:26-27

The *sand* of these verses does not refer to the works of a person whose hope of salvation is in his own human efforts, as some teach. ***It is absolutely necessary to be honest with God's Word!*** To change the meaning of God's plainly written Word is both dishonest and dangerous. Revelation 22:19. The *sand* refers to the failure of this "believer" to make Christ the Lord of His life and to *obey* Him. It is true that we are born again (regenerated) by God, by His Word and by His Spirit working in us. But God does not force an individual to become a "new person in Christ" against his will. And the will cannot be passive. One must have an intense and strong *desire* to *do* God's will. See vss 13-23 and Luke 13:23-27. It is only in the truly sincere person that God can effectively work *to help you first of all to desire and determine to do what is pleasing to Him, and then help you to do it*. Philippians 2:13.

Malachi 3:18 states the following concerning Christ as future judge: "Then you will again see what happens to those who lived righteous lives and to those who lived in sin, to those who served God and to those who didn't." It is vital to realize that the Lord demands obedience and service on the part of those who would be His. Many will have some shocking and terrifying disappointments on that Great Day. But these disappointments will not be the portion of those who, in heeding the warning, become truly converted to Christ. Obviously, people's actions have a great deal to do with their salvation, as indicated by Jesus Himself. If obedience to the Lord is lacking, there will be no salvation for that person, no matter how fine a Christian he may think himself to be. See also Matthew 8:11-12; 10:32-33; 12:36-37; 13:24-30, 36-43; 15:12-14; 16:24-27; 21:42-46; 25:1-46; 1 Corinthians 6:9-10; Galatians 5:19-24; Ephesians 5:5.

201 Matthew 24:29-31

Many Christians believe Christ will have taken His own people to be with Himself before the Great Tribulation. Others believe the Lord will take His own from the earth near the middle of the last seven years of the age, or shortly thereafter. Still others believe that this great event will not take place until Christ returns in power and glory at the Battle of Armageddon, or just previous to that battle, or immediately after. Then there are those who believe that Christ will not call His own to Himself until the moment described in vss 30-31. It would be easiest for the Christians, of course, if the first possibility were correct. How much better to be with the Lord than to go through the Great Tribulation! Those who believe that Christians will go through the Tribulation, or at least through the first part of it, however, have some very convincing Scriptures to support their views.

One of the Scriptures used in support of their contention is 1 Corinthians 15:51-53: "Now listen to me, and I will tell you something that has been a secret: Not all of us will die, but we will all be changed. It will happen in a fraction of a second, in the twinkling of an eye, at the sounding of the last trumpet. Because when that trumpet sounds, all the dead who belong to Christ will be resurrected back to life with bodies that will never die. And we who are still alive will also be changed. Because it's absolutely necessary that these decaying, dying bodies be exchanged for bodies that will never decay or die, that these temporary bodies be exchanged for bodies that are everlasting."

* * *

According to this Scripture the Rapture will take place "at the sounding of the last trumpet." The last trumpet mentioned in the book of The Revelation is the seventh trumpet (Revelation 11:15; 15:1,5 to 16:21) which brings forth the seven vials of the wrath of God upon the earth. The proponents of a mid-tribulation Rapture point out correctly that the seventh trumpet begins to blow in the middle of the last seven years of the age, which period is known as the seven years of the Great Tribulation. The more severe part of the Tribulation will occur during the last three-and-one-half years. It will be a time of tribulation for the nation of Israel, and for all upon earth at that time who are true believers in Christ. But also, the last three-and-one-half years of this seven will be the time of God's judgment upon the ungodly on the earth, and especially at the very end, during the Battle of Armageddon–and following this battle, during the time of darkness, earthquakes, great hailstones, and fire from heaven. Matthew 24:29; Revelation 6:12-14; 2 Thessalonians 1:8; 2 Peter 3:10-12.

This seventh trumpet will very likely continue to blow–at least in the heavens–for three-and-one-half years. Whether or not the sound of the trumpet will be a literal sound upon earth is not revealed. Those who say that the Rapture of the Church will occur in the middle of the seven years believe that the Church will be raptured when this last trumpet begins to blow, or shortly thereafter.

The mid and post tribulationists point out that if the last trumpet spoken of in 1 Corinthians is not the seventh and last trumpet of The Revelation, then there must be a trumpet blast which will follow, because it is definitely called "the last trumpet." If there should be a trumpet to follow the seventh trumpet of The Revelation, the only remaining possibility concerning the timing of the Rapture would be its occurrence after the end of the seven years of the tribulation period.

Another Scripture the mid and post-tribulation rapturists use is 2 Thessalonians 2:1-12. This is a very strong Scripture in their favor. We refer you to the notes on that scripture.

* * *

As to a possible Rapture of the Church before the Tribulation, proponents support their view with such Scriptures as 1 Thessalonians 5:9-10. "Because we know that God has not appointed us to be destroyed by His wrath, but to be saved by means of our Lord Jesus Christ. He died for us, so that whether we are still alert and watchfully living for Him when He comes, or have died in true hope, we will live together with Him forever." Please see the notes on this Scripture, as well.

Returning to v 31 in Matthew 24, people the world over will be included in this great event. Every true child of God who has died since the beginning of time will be resurrected. Every true Christian still living upon the earth will be caught up to be with the Lord. The parable of the good grain and the tares (Matthew 13:30) will thus be fulfilled. The evil will be harvested first (at Armageddon, and in the judgments that follow), and then as described in v 31, the angels will gather the good grain, *God's chosen ones*. Matthew 13:24-30 and 36-40.

Matthew 24:29-31 is one of the main Scriptures presented as evidence by those who believe the Rapture of the Church takes place shortly following the Battle of Armageddon, and just days before God's judgment and renovation of the earth, as described in Revelation 6:12-17. They claim that this is definitely when the last trumpet sounds.

* * *

We can hope to be with the Lord during the time of Great Tribulation on earth; in which case we must make sure that we truly love Him and obey and serve Him, proving that we are truly born again, and are ready to go to be with Him. On the other hand, we must be ready and willing to suffer and die the martyrs death for the sake of our Lord, even today, if such be His will, and especially if we are to go through the Tribulation. Also, we dare not believe in a post-tribulation Rapture of Christ's true Church, and use that as an excuse to put off getting right with the Lord until the Tribulation begins. Because, God's time for you to leave this life may be as soon as today. The *time* of the Rapture is not the all-important thing–getting right with God and being truly born again is what really matters. So be absolutely sure that you are truly born again. If you need help to find your way to God, be sure to read Appendix 245, entitled, The Amazing Story of God.

202 Matthew 25:1-13

The main lesson of this parable of the *ten virgins*, is that many people who consider themselves to be Christians, even waiting for the Lord's coming, will not make it. This is sad indeed. No true follower of Jesus will gloat over such tragedy, but will seek to warn everyone to "be most diligent to make your calling and election to salvation and eternal life with God a sure thing!" 2 Peter 1:10.

The *lamps* and lights of the *five foolish virgins* looked just like those of the *wise virgins*. But the *foolish* had not made any provision to hold firm unto the end (Matthew 24:13), no matter how long or fierce the temptations to live to please ones' self. "The foolish virgins were like the seed that was sown upon the rock. They heard the Word, and at once received it with joy, but they had no root. They were lacking in perseverance, in watchfulness. They did not keep in their minds the thought that, though the bridegroom might come at any moment, still, He might long delay; that there was need for daily preparation, of constant watchfulness for His coming."–Matthew Henry.

In our Lord's parable about the seed sown on the rock (Matthew 13:3-23), the seed was readily accepted by the tiny bit of soil on that rock, but the roots of the seed were never able to penetrate the stony heart. To produce fruit, the seed of the Word of God must be allowed to penetrate deep into the life and soul of a person and take full possession. It is either *all* or *nothing*. If you are holding back any portion of yourself from the Lord, and are unwilling to be faithful and obedient in everything, you are living in rebellion against Him. You are not really converted. Remember, Adam and Eve were rebellious in only one area of their lives. This does not mean that God demands sinless perfection. But He certainly does demand perfect intent.

* * *

Jesus ends this parable with another warning to *watch*. That word *watch* in the Greek means to *not go to sleep, to keep awake*. We must keep awake to everything that would divert our attention away from the Lord and away from the prize. Life everlasting can only be claimed as we are found to be truly in Christ–all the way. Life eternal with our Lord will be so glorious, so wonderful, and so everlasting, that no suffering or pain or waiting can be counted too high a price to pay. Remaining faithful to the end is an absolute imperative. Matthew 10:22; 24:13.

If you have not already done so, promise the Lord this very moment, and from the very depths of your being, to be His totally, in sickness and in health, through all temptations, rejections, or whatever, until you finally stand in His glorious presence. Don't allow any teaching or preaching of *easy believism* to rob you of eternal life. Jesus' warning about false teachers is very applicable today. "Both will fall into a pit"—both the teacher and the one who accepts his message. Matthew 15:14.

203 Matthew 25:14-30

God has entrusted to every one of us certain talents. They consist of abilities, opportunities, money, and whatever other blessings we have or will have in life.

In God's wisdom, and for His own good reasons and purposes, He has given many talents to some, and few talents to others. The person with only one talent is not to be jealous of the person with many. And the one with many talents is not to look down on the person with only one talent.

The person with many talents will have much more for which he will be held accountable to God at The Judgment than the person with only one talent. There will be the temptation to use one's many talents for personal gain, instead of for the glory of God and for the blessing of our fellow-men. Those with the five and the two talents in this parable would surely have been punished comparably to the unfaithful servant with the one talent, if they had invested and used their talents selfishly, or had hidden them in fear. Revelation 21:8.

But, oh, the joy there will be for all who have invested their time and talents wisely and faithfully for the glory of God. One may rightfully ask, "With the end results promised, are you working now as one ought to work, when such ultragreat rewards are obtainable?"

* * *

Each person has at least one talent. If you are a one-talent person, you may be tempted to believe that your little help is not important. But in the first place, what you make of what God has given you is very important to Him. And according to Christ's teaching here, it's very important to your own future as to what you do with whatever you are and have. A person with lesser abilities and opportunities will never know what an impact he can make for God in this world unless he diligently uses the little he now has. God may be giving you a more difficult test with your one talent than those who have many. Don't fail the test, or as surely as you now live, you will receive the judgment Christ warns of here. But if you are faithful to the end, in serving to the extent of your abilities and opportunities, you will receive a reward similar to those who have faithfully served with many talents.

Don't rely on what you've done in the past. Christ says we must be faithful to the end.

The unfaithful servant is seen in the many who want and expect to go to heaven, but they will not go out of their way to serve Christ. If it's easy and pleasant, O.K. But they love their ease and their freedom to do just what they want to do, without concern about the great needs everywhere that could use their involvement.

According to this teaching by Christ, don't count on heaven if you are living at ease and are unfaithful to your responsibilities and opportunities.

* * *

Does this mean you gain heaven by good works? No. But from the beginning God demanded obedience. And when man sinned by disobeying God, He sent His Son, Jesus, to die on the cross for your sins and mine. Now you can be forgiven, because of what Christ has done for you. But the New Testament teaches throughout that after being forgiven you are now to become obedient—not in a few things, but in everything.

In regard to the necessity of obedience to Christ if you are to be saved, look up and read Acts 5:32; Romans 2:6-9; 6:16; 10:9-10; Hebrews 5:9.

Again, "Be most diligent to make your calling and election to salvation and eternal life with God a sure thing!" 2 Peter 1:10.

The whole world is in rebellion against God, and therefore lost! They need to know what you know about Christ and His teachings, and about salvation through Him! According to Matthew 28:18-20, you and I are responsible before God to tell them. Use your talents fully in doing so! And don't stop until your last day on earth! A Christian must never retire from talking to others about their eternity. Romans 10:9-10.

The unfaithful servant was called wicked, and lazy. To be lazy and little concerned about warning the lost is wickedness. And such wickedness will be severely judged by God, to outer darkness. The man's excuse was, "I was afraid." Is that also your excuse for not witnessing? That was the excuse the Israelites used for not obeying God's orders to march in and possess the promised land. And look what happened to them. Numbers 13 and 14. God gives the same warning to cowards today. Revelation 21:8.

Wickedness does not consist in only the wrong you may do. Negative evil—failing or refusing to do what Christ has commanded you to do—is just as sinful. As we see here, it will be judged just as severely. Your reward will be great if you are faithful to the end—but your punishment will be horrendous if you are lazy and disobedient.

* * *

You may think that God's demands are too great, that He's expecting too much. No, He's only demanding right living and right use of what He's given you. And He's promised to always be with you to forgive and to help you live and serve as He demands. You're not on your own. God is always with you to help. See Philippians 2:12-13, and the note there. If you sincerely ask for God's help you can't fail. But you must ask in all sincerity. God bless you! We'll be looking for you in heaven. Bring many with you!

204 Matthew 25:31-46

A great judgment is pictured in these verses, with Jesus Christ seated as Judge. Many have believed this picture to be of the great and final judgment of the wicked. However, since this judgment will take place *when the Son of man comes in His glory*, it cannot be the final judgment of the wicked. Rather, it is the judgment of all persons still alive on the earth at the time of Christ's return. The final judgment of the wicked is to take place at the end of the first thousand years of Christ's reign on earth—the Millennium. Read Revelation 20.

All of God's people who have died will be resurrected to meet Christ in the air *when He returns*, together with those of His who are still alive on the earth. 1 Thessalonians 4:13-18. These will live in the heavenly Jerusalem. Revelation 21:9-27; 22:1-5. So no Christian or Old Testament saint will be included in this judgment, as they will already be with Christ.

As far as the wicked dead are concerned, "The rest of the dead did not come back to life again until the end of the thousand years." Revelation 20:5. It is safe to conclude, then, that sinners who had died before Christ returns will not be included in the judgment described in this Scripture. The final judgment of the wicked dead will come one thousand years later. Revelation 20:11-15.

* * *

It appears quite definitely that the purpose of the judgment mentioned in these verses is to determine who among those still alive on the earth after the Tribulation, and after Christ's true followers have been transported to heaven, are worthy to become subjects in Christ's great new Kingdom on earth. Although *all nations* will be gathered before the Lord for this Judgment, individual persons will be judged on an individual basis. God does not cast entire nations into hell. He saves the righteous among them.

* * *

What criterion will the Lord use at this judgment to judge individuals? The apparent basis will be as to how each one has treated the Lord's *brothers and sisters* during the time of the Great Tribulation. And who are the Lord's *brothers and sisters?* No doubt they will include the Jews and Christians who will go through the Great Tribulation. Even if the Rapture of the Church should take place before the Great Tribulation, there will still be persons converted to Christ during the time of the Tribulation. So it appears that the basis for the Lord's judgment upon these people will be based upon their treatment of the Jews and Christians during that last terrible time of testing.

The Lord does not promise heaven to these friends of the Jews and Christians on the basis of their friendship. Only as these individuals are converted to Christ as Lord and Savior during the Millenium is it probable that eternal life will be theirs. Jesus' words to them are, "Come, you who are blessed by My Father, and inherit the Kingdom that was prepared for you from the time that the world was created." God's Kingdom on earth will not be peopled, as we have mentioned, by those who are with the Lord in the heavenly Jerusalem. But the earth will be repopulated by those who had been good to God's people, and who had not taken the mark of the beast (Revelation 13:16-18; 14:9-11), during the time of the reign of the Satan-inspired man, the Antichrist.

* * *

The individuals sent from the Lord's presence *into everlasting fire* at this time will be those who had mistreated the Jews and Christians during the time of the Great Tribulation, or had refused to help them. They will be the people who had cooperated with Antichrist and had received his mark on their hand or forehead. As the Scriptures warn, no one who receives this mark and cooperates with Antichrist will have any part in God's Kingdom. Revelation 14:9-11 states, "And another angel, a third one, followed them, loudly shouting, 'Here's what will happen to anyone who worships the beast and his image, and receives his mark on his hand or forehead: He will be included among those who will drink of the wine of God's furious anger, which has been poured out full strength into the cup of His boiling fury. And he will be tormented with fire and burning sulphur in the presence of the holy angels and of the Lamb. And the smoke of their torment will rise up forever and ever. Day after endless day and night after endless night they will have no rest. This awful judgment will fall upon all who worship the beast and his image, and upon all who receive his mark or his name.'"

* * *

It will be difficult, if not next to impossible, to buy or sell through ordinary channels during part or all of the Tribulation period without the mark of the beast. But to accept that mark, will ultimately result in judgment and hell. The reign of Antichrist, "the beast", will be anti-God, anti-Christ, anti-Jew, and anti-Christian. And God warns that anyone who has any part with the Antichrist–accepting his mark or number in their forehead or in their right hand for the necessary and legitimate purposes of doing business, or even of sustaining life, will lose his soul. See also Daniel 7:9-10; Malachi 3:1-5; Mark 6:11; Jude 3-4, 13-15.

The *eternal life* received by those who are declared *righteous* at this judgment will no doubt be eternal life on the earth, but not in the heavenly Jerusalem. Revelation 21:9-27; 22:1-5. At least, this is the immediate promise Christ will give them.

205 Matthew 13:1-23; Mark 4:1-20; Luke 8:4-15.

Consider what the Lord is saying here in the parable about the farmer sowing seed. The one sowing seed is any minister, Bible teacher, or anyone else telling one or more people the Great News God has for them.

Those receiving the message along the hard pathway are those who hear the message, but their hard hearts won't allow the message to change them. They try as quickly as possible to forget it, especially if they were convicted by it. Some of these folks even attend church regularly. They attend mainly for social reasons. They have little interest in the truth. They think only of their own selfish plans and desires.

Such hearts need to be plowed deeply by uncompromising preaching, backed by much prayer by preacher and people. There needs to be a breaking up and crushing of the heart in order to get the seed in where it can grow. If those with hard hearts have any concern at all for their future in heaven or hell, they also need to pray.

The writer of these notes is experienced in this area. I was a hypocrite. I was an active church member, and listened to the preached message every week. But nothing changed. I really didn't have desire to change, although I knew I should. Finally, after many years, I prayed, "Lord, I know what I should do, but I'm not willing. I seem to be helpless. But I'm willing for You to make me willing." God answered my prayer. It cost me plenty to be crushed, but the blessed assurance I now have in Christ is worth it all.

* * *

Those who receive the seed in the thin soil on the rock are those who joyfully accept the message, but can't take the heat when persecution comes. They are more concerned about keeping their old friends who are on their way to hell, and more concerned about pleasing family members than in pleasing the Lord. They want heaven, but not if it's going to cost them very much.

Some of this is due to faulty preaching and teaching. Jesus always let His hearers know that it would cost them everything to follow Him and gain eternal life. Too many preachers and teachers are preaching an easy way to heaven. The way is not easy, it's hard! Matthew 7:13-14. But every step of the difficult way will be worth it when we get where we are going, instead of where the others are going.

* * *

Those who receive the message among thorns are those who agree with the message. The Greek word for "hear" in this instance has been translated "continue to listen" because it's in the present active, denoting continuous action.

They are people who agree with the message, are baptized, become church members, and even serve the Lord. But they are slaves to their daily cares, and are cumbered with desire for wealth and for all in this life that will satisfy their carnal appetites.

The work they do for the Lord is done mainly to ease their conscience. They would rather spend their time "in a more profitable and enjoyable way." So the work they do for God is not from the heart and is not very effective. They don't produce a crop.

Give heed to Christ's warning to such people in John 15:1-6. Christ demands our all, nothing less. You cannot be only half converted and be converted. You may object and say that that's not the way Rev. or Dr. So and So preaches and teaches. But it is the way Christ and His apostles taught! Check it out. Read the Book for yourself and let God show you what the truth is.

Don't let the cares of this world and the desire for things and experiences bog you down and bring upon you the judgment received by those in John 15:1-6.

Be one of those in Mark 4:20. The Greek word for "hear" in this verse is also translated "continue to listen," because it's also in the present active, indicating continuous present action. But it's also in the indicative mood, which is the mood of certainty. These folks have a positive attitude about the message of the Lord. They really believe it, and live it.

They put obedience to God ahead of all else. And they are constantly searching His Word so they may obey and serve Him better. Anything that hinders or keeps them from being their best for the Lord is put out of their lives, or they turn it completely over to the Lord, trusting Him to make it to be a blessing instead of a hindrance. They are living for God, and for eternal treasures. They are thoroughly enjoying the present, in spite of the difficulties, as they serve the Lord, in whatever occupation they are in. But their sights are on the eternal future!

No wonder God is blessing, and they are producing a great harvest. Join these dedicated ones with all your heart! Fearful warnings from Christ and His apostles hang over all others! Not on just some of the others, but on all the others!

The Amazing Story of God

245 There was a time when there was nothing; no trees, no flowers, birds, animals, or even people–nothing. There wasn't even an earth, or sun, moon, or stars–nothing–nothing but God!

The overwhelmingly greatest thing we discover about God as we read the Bible is that He is a God of love. Yes, there are times when God expresses Himself in fierce anger and judgment, but He does so only when it's the right thing to do. Even we do right when we become angry because of some wrong that's being done, and take the necessary steps to correct it.

Why a Son?

In several places the Bible states that *God is love*. The fact that God is a God of love is also both stated and implied in many other places throughout Scripture. And from experience we know that if we have love in our hearts, we need someone to love. And with a heart of love such as God has, his desire was to have others like Himself whom He could love and who would love Him in return. The first act of God that we know anything about was when He fathered a Son. We are not told how God did this, we are simply told that He has a Son whom He fathered before anything was created.

The Son is from eternity the same as the Father. But it's just as difficult for us creatures of time to fully understand eternity as it is for us to really understand God. Maybe this truth has been best stated by the *original* Westminster Confession of Faith which very simply states, "The Son of God was begotten of the Father from eternity." One of the other confessions of faith says, "He was begotten, not made." We have been created, but the One we speak of here was begotten (born) of the Father. Don't ask how the Father did this. The Bible doesn't reveal how. But it does reveal that God has a begotten Son.

The ancient Athanasian Creed states that He is "of the substance of the Father, begotten before the worlds." The Nicene Creed states that He was "begotten of His Father before all the worlds."[1]

And for God to receive love in the measure that He could give, He needed someone who was like Himself, who could love Him with the same measure that He could love. So God gave His Son all the glory, power, and capabilities that He Himself has.[2] The Son of God is just like the Father. He has the same capacity for love, the same wisdom, the same power, etc. So the Son is also God.[3]

Still, there is only one Supreme God, which is the Father.[4] And because the Son always does what pleases the Father, they are one God in unity. There is no clashing of personalities between the Father and the Son. The Son never has and never will try to overthrow the Father and take the Father's place.[5]

It was sometime after the Son received His power and glory from the Father that creation was begun. And everything God created He created through His Son.[6] His Son did all the actual creating of all things everywhere. Nothing that has been created has been created by anyone except by the Son. Just as good human fathers rejoice in what their sons can do, evidently God receives the same satisfaction in seeing what His Son can do.

God's many sons

But God's love is so great that He wants to love and be loved by many sons and daughters. So in the very first chapter of the Bible you will find that God made mankind just like Himself, to be His children. He created man in His own image and likeness. We're not merely a superior species of the animal world; we are made in the image of God to be His children! And God's purpose from the beginning was that His children would not only be like Him but also that they would be with Him and share His glory. This is still God's plan. God isn't finished with us yet in bringing us to our ultimate likeness to Himself. For just a few Scriptures regarding our future glory, look up and read Romans 5:2; 8:18; 1 Corinthians 15:43; Hebrews 2:10; 1 Peter 5:1.

The rebellion

However, Adam and Eve, God's first created children, took things into their own hands and decided to please themselves instead of obeying their Father. And every last one of us has done the same thing. We have all sinned and come short of the glory of God.[7] God warned His children that if they disobeyed Him they would die. And this happened, and is continuing to happen. But this dying is not only physical death but spiritual death.[8] Being created in the image of God we are eternal spirits, just as God is. We will always be somewhere. But those who continue in their rebellion toward their heavenly Father will be separated from God in an awful state of punishment for untold ages to come.

God is loving and kind, but He can't let us into heaven for only those reasons. It would be impossible for God to simply say, "Well, we'll just forget about all the times you've ignored and disobeyed Me and lived to please yourself instead of Me. I forgive you." If God's nature was such that His great love was greater than His wisdom and righteousness, and we could gain His forgiveness whenever we chose, His entire Kingdom would fall. Because then we could know that we could always do just as we pleased, and ask His forgiveness whenever we needed His pardon; and then continue in our rebellion, because we could always be forgiven. But God's love is so great that He earnestly wants to forgive, and He devised a way to do so in wisdom and righteousness.

God's plan—a Savior

The way the Father made it possible for Himself to offer us forgiveness, in a legal and righteous way, and still preserve His Kingdom, was to send His incomparable Son, the One who created us–sending Him to earth in human form to become one of us. We know Him as Jesus Christ, the One who came to earth in human form some two thousand years ago.

If someone ridicules you for believing in Jesus Christ, give him this information: Jesus is no fictional character; it's a historical fact that He lived in Israel some 2,000 years ago. At thirty years of age He went public about who He was. He claimed to be the Son of God. He said the Father had sent Him to earth in human form on a mission, and with a message for mankind.[9]

* * *

He made many other claims about Himself, which only a fool or a con man would make, unless they were true. Some refuse to acknowledge Him as the Son of God and the Savior of the world, but acknowledge He was the greatest teacher and the most godly man who ever lived. But you can't have it both ways. Either He was all He claimed to be, or He was the greatest liar, deceiver, or fool that ever walked the face of this earth. But He proved in many amazing ways that He was all He claimed to be!

In the first place, The Father had sent prophets to Israel for over a thousand years telling them that the Christ (the Messiah) was coming. He even told them where He would be born (in Bethlehem),[10] that He would have no human father, but would be born of a virgin.[11] He even told them that later His Father, God, would call Him out of Egypt.[12]

Jesus was born to be King of Israel. You would think that a king would enter the capital city riding triumphantly upon a horse. But Zechariah 9:9 prophesied that the Messiah would humbly enter Jerusalem riding upon a donkey and upon the colt of a donkey. You will find the fulfillment of that reported in Matthew 21:1-7, together with an informative note. There are hundreds of prophecies in the Old Testament about His coming, and about what would happen when He came.

Miraculous proof

His miraculous life was further proof. He healed the sick, the lame, blind, deaf, dumb, the palsied. He turned water into wine, stopped storms, walked on water, raised the dead, fed over 5,000 men (besides women and children) with only five small loaves of bread and two small fish. Afterward He had His followers gather up the leftover scraps, and they collected 12 basketsful! That was much more than He had started out with. He was untouchable when a crowd tried to throw Him over a cliff. He even prophesied His own death and how He would die. He prophesied that His own people, the Jews, would turn Him over to the Romans to be crucified.

His greatest prophecy, and the fulfillment of it, was that He would rise back to life again three days after He died! His followers saw Him die. They watched as the Roman soldier plunged the spear into His side, resulting in blood and water flowing out. Those same followers later went throughout the then-known world telling the Great News about the Savior, that He had died and had come back to life, and now lives. And that because He lives, we too can now live forever.

He was seen by His followers at various intervals for forty days after His resurrection. Some 500 of them saw Him at one time. After forty days He ascended into the heavens as His followers watched. Then two angels appeared and told them, "You men from Galilee, why are you standing here staring into the sky? This Jesus, who has just been taken from you into heaven, will return in the very same way you watched Him go into heaven."

He's coming again–this time as King of kings and Lord of lords! And the prophecy in Zechariah 12:10-14 is that the Jewish nation "will look on Me whom they have pierced." The prophet goes on to tell how the Jewish nation will then go into deep mourning as they realize what they had done to their Messiah when they crucified Him.

* * *

Possibly the greatest proof that Jesus is indeed the Son of God was the perfect life He lived. Quoting from Isaiah 53:9, the apostle Peter wrote concerning Him, "He never committed a sin. Not even one lie came out of His mouth." The apostle John said concerning His sinlessness, "You all know that the Lord Jesus appeared among us to take away our sins. And not even once did He disobey God." These men could say these things about Him after living with Him constantly for over three years! Christ was the first and only Man who ever lived without sin. He lived the only perfect life ever lived.

But He allowed himself to be horribly tortured, and then crucified on a cross by cruel men. He allowed all this so that He, the Son of God, might suffer, and shed His blood, and die, because of our sins. He, our Creator, took awful punishment in our place!

A pardon offered

Now God is able (in wisdom and righteousness) to offer us forgiveness, if we will accept it on the condition that we turn from our sin to obedience to Him. That's what being born again is all about. You may have heard the Scripture which states, "Because God's love for the people of this world is so great, He gave His incomparable Son, so that whoever is believing in Him may not perish, but have life that will never end."[13]

As we have stated, God has wonderful plans for His children. He doesn't want any of them to be lost. He wants all of them to be saved. But all have freedom of will. We can choose to turn from our sin and obey God, and receive His forgiveness and eternal life, or we can choose to continue to go our own way and suffer the consequences of a horrendous hell, and after that the Lake of Fire. Revelation 20:11-15.

A legitimate concern

One main concern that keeps people from accepting God's forgiveness and turning their life over to Him is that they believe they can't hold out. That's a legitimate concern. However, Jesus promised those who truly follow Him that He will always be with them to help them. Matthew 28:20. The Apostle Paul states in Philippians 2:13, "Because God is always at work within you, helping you first of all to desire and determine to do what is pleasing to Him, and then helping you to do it." For some vital comments on that Scripture see Appendix 218.

The aim of every Christian must be to please God perfectly. But none of us are perfect in this life. There are times when we fail, and we must come to the Lord again and then again and ask His forgiveness. Someone so rightly said, "The Christian life is a series of new beginnings." The Apostle John wrote a letter to Christians which is called 1 John in the New Testament, and in vss 8 and 9 of chapter 1 of that letter we read, "If we say we never sin, we're only fooling ourselves, and there's no truth whatever in our claim. But, if we humbly and sincerely make a practice of confessing our sins to God when we have failed Him, He will be faithful and true to His promise to forgive us our sins and to cleanse us from all the selfish and immoral things we have done."

That doesn't mean we have license to sin, but that when we do stumble and fall on our face God is willing to forgive again because of the sacrifice Christ made for our sins. But let's never forget that our aim must be perfection. But when we fail, our God who loves us so dearly desires to forgive us and help us to get going for Him again. So don't wait until you are able to live a perfect life (for none of us are perfect), but accept God's forgiveness now and surrender your life totally to Him. You will then have the joy in this life of knowing that the Lord is with you, and the assurance that all is well for all eternity. It would be wise for you to turn to 1 John right now and read the first chapter (only ten verses). Also read the brief notes there.

Then consider the following:

Where's the profit?

One day when Jesus was on earth He said to His followers, "What good would it all do you even if you gained all the wealth and power and all the flesh-fulfilling experiences in all the world, but then found yourself barred from heaven and sent to your judgment in hell? Or look at it this way: If you suddenly found yourself suffering in hell, how much would you then be willing to give of yourself to God in order to gain His forgiveness and eternal life?"[14] Think that over for a moment. In hell you will have no opportunity whatever to be born again spiritually, to be converted from living in sin and living as you please, to living for God. There will be absolutely no hope in hell. And no exit! Right NOW is the only time you are sure of having in which you can surrender your heart and life to God, and begin living in obedience to Him. God isn't asking too much, He's only asking that you accept His forgiveness and give Him your obedience like any child should obey a father who loves him so much.

A wise man once said, "You cannot run a society or cope with its problems if people are not held accountable for what they do." And God cannot run a world if His children are not held accountable for what they do. It's only right that you accept the forgiveness your Father offers you, and then live to please Him.

Most of the people of this world are in sad condition. And the more determined people are to disregard God and go their own way, the worse their condition gets. But God wants to change all that in your life, and give you peace and joy and the sure hope of everlasting life with Him. He has such wonderful plans for you for all eternity. Will you accept His love and forgiveness before you are forever lost?

A preview of hell

To be lost from God, loved ones, and heaven, will mean to be abandoned in the fearful and awful place of torment that the Bible calls hell. The Bible so very definitely tells us about the absolute fact of hell and the horrors of it. Consider just one warning that Jesus gave about hell in the 16th chapter of Luke, where He told about a rich man who went to hell.

From Jesus' own words here we are told that hell is a place of horrendous torment, where those who have ignored God and have refused to obey Him will be punished. There is a great gulf fixed between hell and heaven, so that no one can go from one place to the other. Once a person is in hell, there is no escape. Also, it will be impossible to commit suicide in hell.

We learn that the suffering will be great. It's represented by torment in a flame of fire. It will nevertheless be a dark, obscure, and miserable place, where the wicked will be punished with no glimmer of hope of ever being released.

All indications are that those in hell will be able to see the joy and glory they could have experienced forever in heaven. See Revelation 14:10. To see where you could have been will only add to your anguish and despair.

The rich man asks that a poor beggar he sees in heaven be allowed to come and give him at least one drop of cool water, but even that is not possible. There will be no relief whatever, not even for a brief moment. There won't be even a one minute recess.

And one of the greatest sufferings in hell will be one's memory. They will remember when they refused God's forgiveness and the offer of eternal life. And the reason most folks will be in hell is because they have loved some sin which they were unwilling to give up.

No one plans to go to hell. Most who are there now planned to get right with God, someday. Maybe tomorrow, or next week, but that tomorrow never came. They always wanted freedom to indulge in their sin a little longer.

As an outstanding servant of God has stated: "There is no sin, no matter how pleasurable–and sin can be pleasurable–that is worth the awful consequences."[15]

The loss would be incalculable!

Also, think of all the joys you will miss if you miss heaven. There will be perfect love there. No disappointments. There will be perfect fulfillment in every way, resulting in perfect joy. In fact, in Psalm 16:11 we are told that in God's presence we will experience fullness of joy, and pleasures forevermore.

Are the unfulfilling and unsatisfactory pleasures of this brief and uncertain life, and everything else here that's coming to nothing, worth hanging on to at the expense of losing out on an eternal life in heaven with your real Father who loves you so? Don't wait another day, or even another moment, to make sure of being with your real family in heaven.

Decide for heaven, for sure

Will you sincerely make the following prayer *your* prayer?

Dear God, my Father:

I am so sorry I have fought You for control of the throne of my life, and have insisted on living my life as I've pleased, instead of living it to please You. There is so much I've done that I'm ashamed of and so much I haven't done. I have been so wrong in going my own way and ignoring You. I've been selfishly concerned about only pleasing myself when I've rebelliously resisted Your leadership.

But I'm coming to You now even though I know I'm not a pretty sight. I am dirty with the impurities of my sin. Thank You for loving me anyway and for sending Jesus to suffer and die in my place as the sin-offering for my sin. I now accept Him into my life to take full control of it as my Lord and my Savior.

Lord Jesus, I welcome You–be born in me right here, right now. You can have whatever is left of my life, and I will continually look to You for help and strength to live to please You. I love You for loving me so much. Help me now to love You and others as You have loved me. Amen.

* * *

God's Kingdom has a most wonderful

future, and you can be a part of it in a most wonderful way. Don't miss it! The alternative is too awful to even consider as a possibility.

After you have accepted God's gift of Life, find a good church where the pastor and people really love, serve, and obey God. Don't settle for a lukewarm fellowship. You need to be with people who really love God. But don't expect a perfect church. Perfection won't come until we are with the Lord.

When you have found your church fellowship, ask the pastor about being baptized. One of your first acts of obedience to the Lord should be your baptism. In your baptism you let the world and all of heaven know that you now belong to Jesus. And in your baptism you are testifying that you are burying your old life and rising up to live a new life for Christ and for God, your Father. Romans 6:1-8.

If all are lost, all need to hear

When you have accepted God's love and forgiveness, tell others how they, too, may be saved. Not everyone will be glad to listen, but some will. And even where you get only a few words in, that may be the very seed that will eventually lead that person to turn from sin, to believe and be saved.

God has made every follower of the Lord Jesus responsible to tell and warn others. If you are lost without the Savior, so are all others, and they need to know what you know in order to be saved. One of the tests of obedience that God gives is stated in the Scripture that says:

"If you will speak out and share with others what you know and believe about the Lord Jesus, and if you sincerely believe in your heart that God has indeed raised Him from the dead, you will be saved. Because it's when you are sincerely believing with your heart that you gain right standing with God. So when as a result of true heart-belief you make a practice of opening your mouth to talk to others about the Lord Jesus, the result will include your own salvation."[16]

God bless and use you now for His glory and the salvation of many others.

References for The Amazing Story of God:

1. John 1:1-4; 17:5,24; Colossians 1:17.
2. John 17:24; 1 Corinthians 15:24-28.
3. John 1:1; Hebrews 1:7-8.
4. John 17:3; 1 Corinthians 8:6; Ephesians 4:6.
5. 1 Corinthians 15:24-28.
6. John 1:3; Ephesians 3:9c; Colossians 1:15-16; Hebrews 1:1-2.
7. Romans 3:23.
8. Revelation 20:11-15.
9. John 8:23-30; 12:44-50; 20:21
10. Micah 5:2; Matthew 2:1-6.
11. Isaiah 7:14; Luke 1:26-38; Matthew 1:18-25.
12. Hosea 11:1; Matthew 2:13-21
13. John 3:16.
14. Mark 8:36-37.
15. Galatians 6:7-8.
16. Romans 10:9-10.